(get context

"... leaves us just on the level with the most ignorant as to what the Divine Spirit actually is in itself." p. 305

comparison to levels of understanding electricity

BIBLE MYSTERY
AND
BIBLE MEANING

"What may be the nature of the Divine self-consciousness in itself is a matter on which we can in no way profitably speculate ..."

p. 191

"... all we can know of God is our own consciousness of our relation to him ..."

p. 191

Also by Thomas Troward
and published by DeVorss

THE EDINBURGH AND DORÉ LECTURES
(single-volume edition with notes)

THE CREATIVE PROCESS IN THE INDIVIDUAL

COLLECTED ESSAYS OF THOMAS TROWARD
(originally *The Hidden Power*)

THE LAW AND THE WORD

BIBLE MYSTERY AND BIBLE MEANING

Thomas Troward

Fides et Amor Veritas et Robur

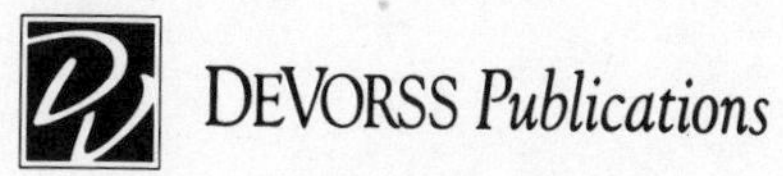

Bible Mystery and Bible Meaning

ISBN: 0-87516-647-4
Third Printing, 2000

DeVorss & Company, Publisher
P.O. Box 550
Marina del Rey, CA 90294

Printed in The United States of America

CONTENTS

A WORD FROM THE PUBLISHER vii

1. THE CREATION 1
2. THE FALL 26
3. ISRAEL 44
4. THE MISSION OF MOSES 77
5. THE MISSION OF JESUS 105
6. THE BUILDING OF THE TEMPLE 126
7. THE SACRED NAME 157
8. THE DEVIL 197
9. THE LAW OF LIBERTY 214
10. THE TEACHING OF JESUS 232
11. THE FORGIVENESS OF SIN 267
12. FORGIVENESS, ITS RELATION TO HEALING AND TO THE STATE OF THE DEPARTED IN THE OTHER WORLD 282
13. THE DIVINE GIVING 299
14. THE SPIRIT OF ANTICHRIST 314

A Word from the Publisher

The study of *Bible Mystery and Bible Meaning* is especially rewarding to the student of Mental Science for the further light it sheds on the philosophy of Thomas Troward as first given in his *Edinburgh Lectures on Mental Science* (1904), which preceded the greater part of the present work by only a year. Thus, although formally conceived as an introduction to the study of the Bible (and not as a commentary on it), *Bible Mystery and Bible Meaning* is a very rich elaboration of the themes of the earlier book, pursuing these into new byways of interest and reflection that lend point to the observation by Harry Gaze, Troward's friend and memoirist, that the study of all of Troward's works becomes, for the serious student, "a gradual necessity."

"The whole Bible," Troward tells us, "is a commentary on the text, 'Man is the image and likeness of God' "; indeed, Troward never drops this thread however widely he ranges in thought. And many of

Troward's most interesting reflections are best presented here—some of them *only* here. Socially conscious, he examines our situation in terms of its outward correspondence to the inward mental state of the masses of mankind. Metaphysical environmentalism surfaces as he discusses the effect of the spiritual condition of the human race upon Nature as a whole. Here too is Troward on weapons of mass destruction ("the glorious games of murder with the latest modern appliances"). Evil is sensitively and compellingly seen in terms of the disintegration of our individuality in either person or circumstances. He also discusses the notorious "latter days," which many target for the end of this century.

Yet there is room in Mental Science for Divine "pardon" and "reconciliation"—Troward explains how, as well as the fascinating truth of *"our simultaneous existence on the supreme plane of Spirit"* even as we live Earth life. And as for that: could there be a case for a "prenatal subjective consciousness" of a law of *heredity* governing the formation of "the People of the I AM"? Read, too, Troward on whether Spirit "gave Itself to death" for us in the person of Jesus Christ; on whether there is any necessity for dying—and why; on discarnate spirits, gurus and other middlemen, the key to social harmony, Jesus' greatest teaching, the Chosen People, the afterlife and some problems, the "Latter Days," the Antichrist. Nor is this all.

Eight years after the first appearance of *Bible Mystery and Bible Meaning* (1905), several chapters were added. The student of Troward's thought will find great interest in the distance traveled between the end of Chapter 10 (emphasizing the Bible as "a statement of the working of Laws") and the opening of Chapter 11, with its warning of "an erroneous course of reasoning resulting in logical conclusions the very opposite of all that the Bible is seeking to teach us"—in other words, the "calamity" of recognizing "a spiritual power of mere *forces*" without seeing beyond this "the presence of 'the God of gods.' " This, taken in the context of the final chapter ("The Spirit of Antichrist") and what we know of Troward's religious sentiments in the closing years of his life (he died in 1916), raises important questions about "the distance traveled" by him in, and possibly beyond, Mental Science.

DeVorss & Company's commitment to the works of Thomas Troward is based on an awareness of their continuing importance and on a desire to see them available to the public at affordable prices. And as reissues are often opportunities, we have seized this one of correcting misprints and other errors; introducing judicious paragraphing where paragraphs were intimidatingly and unjustifiably long; adding or changing punctuation to conform to current style, easing the work of reading; and providing footnote aids where names, words, and phrases were unlikely to be known to the reader.

If, as Troward tells us at the very outset, the Bible is the Book of the Emancipation of Man, then *Bible Mystery and Bible Meaning* is the book par excellence of our enlightenment in the study of the Bible. DeVorss & Company re-presents it with very great pride.

ARTHUR VERGARA
Editor

BIBLE MYSTERY

AND

BIBLE MEANING

CHAPTER 1

The Creation

THE BIBLE is the Book of Emancipation of Man. The emancipation of man means his deliverance from sorrow and sickness, from poverty, struggle, and uncertainty, from ignorance and limitation, and finally from death itself. This may appear to be what the euphemistic* colloquialism of the day would call "a tall order," but nevertheless it is impossible to read the Bible with a mind unwarped by antecedent conceptions derived from traditional interpretation without seeing that this is exactly what it promises, and that it professes to contain the secret whereby this happy condition of perfect liberty may be attained.

Jesus says that if a man keeps his saying, he shall never see death (John 8:51); in the Book of Job we

*Previous editions show *euphuistic*, which does not, however, appear to be supported by the context. —*Ed.*

are told that if a man has with him "a messenger, an interpreter," he shall be delivered from going down to the pit, and shall return to the days of his youth (Job 33:23–25); the Psalms speak of our renewing our youth (Psalm 103:5); and yet again we are told in Job that by acquainting ourselves with God we shall be at peace, we shall lay up gold as dust and have plenty of silver, we shall decree a thing and it shall be established unto us (Job 22:21–28).

Now, what I propose is that we shall reread the Bible on the supposition that Jesus and these other speakers really meant what they said. Of course, from the standpoint of the traditional interpretation this is a startling proposition. The traditional explanation assumes that it is impossible for these things to be literally true, and therefore it seeks some other meaning in the words, and so gives them a "spiritual" interpretation.

But in the same manner we may spiritualize away an Act of Parliament; and it hardly seems the best way of getting at the meaning of a book to follow the example of the preacher who commenced his discourse with the words, "Beloved brethren, the text doth not mean what it saith." Let us, however, start with the supposition that these texts do mean what they say, and try to interpret the Bible on these lines. It will at least have the attraction of novelty; and I think if the reader gives his careful attention to the following pages, he will see that this method carries with it the conviction of reason.

If a thing is true at all, there is a *way* in which it is true, and when the *way* is seen, we find that to be perfectly reasonable which, before we understood the way, appeared unreasonable. We all go by railroad now, yet they were esteemed level-headed practical men in their day who proposed to confine George Stephenson* as a lunatic for saying that it was possible to travel at thirty miles an hour.

The first thing to notice is that there is a common element running through the texts I have quoted; they all contain the idea of acquiring certain information, and the promised results are all contingent on our getting this information, and using it. Jesus says it depends on our keeping his saying, that is, receiving the information which he had to give and acting upon it. Job says that it depends on rightly interpreting a certain message, and again that it depends on our making ourselves acquainted with something; and the context of the passage in the Psalms makes it clear that the deliverance from death and the renewal of youth there

*(1781-1848), English inventor and founder of railroads —*Ed.*

promised are to be attained through the "ways" which the Lord "made known unto Moses."

In all these passages we find that these wonderful results come from the attainment of certain knowledge, and the Bible therefore appeals to our Reason. From this point of view we may speak of the Science of the Bible, and as we advance in our study, we shall find that this is not a misuse of terms, for the Bible is eminently scientific; only its science is not primarily physical but mental.

The Bible contemplates Man as composed of "Spirit, soul, and body" (1 Thess. 5:23), or in other words as combining into a single unity a threefold nature—spiritual, psychic, and corporeal; and the knowledge which it proposes to give us is the knowledge of the true relation between these three factors. The Bible also contemplates the totality of all Being, manifested and unmanifested, as likewise constituting a threefold unity, which may be distributed under the terms "God," "Man," and "the Universe"; and it occupies itself with telling us of the interaction, both positive and negative, which goes on between these three. Furthermore, it bases this interaction upon two great psychological laws, namely, that of the creative power of Thought and that of the amenability of Thought to control by Suggestion; and it affirms that this Creative Power is as innately inherent in Man's Thought as in the Divine Thought.

But it also shows how through ignorance of these truths we unknowingly misuse our creative power, and so produce the evils we deplore; and it also realizes the extreme danger of recognizing our power before we have attained the moral qualities which will fit us to use it in accordance with those principles which keep the great totality of things in an abiding harmony; and to avoid this danger, the Bible veils its ultimate meaning under symbols, allegories, and parables.

But these are so framed as to reveal this ultimate meaning to those who will take the trouble to compare the various statements with one another, and who are sufficiently intelligent to draw the deductions which follow from thus putting two and two together; while those who cannot thus read between the lines are trained into the requisite obedience to the Universal Law by means of suggestions suited to the present extent of their capacity, and are thus gradually prepared for the fuller recognition of the Truth as they advance.

Seen in this light, the Bible is found not to be a mere collection of old-world fables or unintelligible dogmas, but a statement of great universal laws, all of which proceed simply and naturally from the initial truth that Creation is a process of Evolution. Grant the evolutionary theory, which every advance in modern science renders clearer, and all the rest follows, for the entire Bible is based upon the principle of Evolution. But the Bible is a statement of Universal Law, of that which obtains in the realm of the invisible as well as that which obtains in the realm of the visible, and therefore it deals with facts of a transcendental nature as well as with those of the physical plane; and accordingly it contemplates an earlier process anterior to Evolution—the process, namely, of Involution: the passing of Spirit into Form as antecedent to the passing of Form into Consciousness. If we bear this in mind, it will throw light on many passages which must remain wrapped in impenetrable obscurity until we know something of the psychic principles to which they refer.

The fact that the Bible always contemplates Evolution as necessarily preceded by Involution should never be lost sight of, and therefore much of the Bible requires to be read as referring to the involutionary process taking place upon the psychic plane. But Involution and Evolution are not opposed to one another; they are only the earlier and later stages of the same process: the perpetual urging onward of Spirit for Self-expression in infinite varieties of Form. And therefore the grand foundation on which the whole Bible system is built up is that the Spirit, which is thus continually passing into manifesation, is always the *same* Spirit. In other words, it is only ONE.

These two fundamental truths—that under whatever varieties of Form, the Spirit is only ONE; and that the creation of all *forms*, and consequently of the whole world of *conscious relations*, is the result of Spirit's ONE mode of action, which is Thought—are the basis of all that the Bible has to teach us, and therefore from its first page to its last, we shall find these two ideas continually recurring in a variety of different connections: the ONEness of the Divine Spirit and the Creative Power of Man's Thought, which the Bible expresses in its two grand statements, that "God is ONE," and that Man is made "in the image and likeness of God."

These are the two fundamental statements of the Bible, and all its other statements flow logically from them. And since the whole argument of Scripture is built up from these premises, the reader must not be surprised at the frequency with which our analysis of that argument will bring us back to these two initial propositions. So far from being a vain repetition, this continual reduction of the statements of the Bible to the premises with which it originally sets out is the strongest proof that we have in them a sure and solid foundation on which to base our present life and our future expectations.

But there is yet another point of view from which the Bible appears to be the very opposite of a logically accurate system built up on the broad foundations of Natural Law. From this point of view it at first looks like the egotistical and arrogant tradition of a petty tribe, the narrow book of a narrow sect, instead of a statement of Universal Truth; and yet this aspect of it is so prominent that it can by no means be ignored. It is impossible to read the Bible and shut our eyes to the fact that it tells us of God making a covenant with Abraham, and thenceforward separating his descendants by a divine interposition from the remainder of mankind; for this separation of a certain portion of the race as special objects of the Divine favour forms an integral part of Scripture from the story of Cain and Abel to the description of "the camp of the saints and the beloved city" in the Book of Revelation.

We cannot separate these two aspects of the Bible, for they are so interwoven with one another that if we attempt to do so, we shall end by having no Bible left, and we are therefore compelled to accept the Bible statement as a whole or reject it altogether, so that we are met by the paradox of a combination between an all-inclusive system of

Natural Law and an exclusive selection which at first appears to flatly contradict the processes of Nature. Is it possible to reconcile the two?

The answer is that it is not only possible, but that this exclusive selection is the necessary consequence of the Universal Law of Evolution when working in the higher phases of individualism. It is not that those who do not come within the pale of this Selection suffer any diminution, but that those who do come within it receive thereby a special augmentation, and, as we shall see by and by, this takes place by a purely natural process resulting from the more intelligent employment of that knowledge which it is the purpose of the Bible to unfold to us.

These two principles of the inclusive and the exclusive are intertwined in a double thread which runs all through Scripture, and this dual nature of its statements must always be borne in mind if we would apprehend its meaning. Asking the reader, therefore, to carefully go over these preliminary remarks as affording the clue to the *reason* of the Bible statements, I shall now turn to the first chapter of Genesis.

The opening announcement that "in the beginning God created the heaven and the earth" contains the statement of the first of those two propositions which are the fundamental premises from which the whole Bible is evolved. From the Master's instruction to the woman of Samaria we know that "God" means "Spirit"; not "*a* Spirit," as in the Authorised* Version, thus narrowing the Divine Being with the limitations of individuality, but as it stands in the original Greek, simply "Spirit"—that is, *all* Spirit, or Spirit in the Universal. Thus the opening words of the Bible may be read, "in the beginning Spirit"—which is a statement of the underlying Universal Unity.

Here let me draw attention to the twofold meaning of the words "in the beginning." They may mean *first in order of time*, or *first in order of causation*, and the latter meaning is brought out by the Latin version, which commences with the words "*in principio*"—that is, "in principle." This distinction should be borne in mind, for in all subsequent stages of evolution the initial principle which gives rise to the individualized entity must still be in operation as the *fons et origo*† of that particular manifestation just as much as in its first concentration; it is the root of the individuality, without which the individuality would cease to exist. It is the "beginning" of the individuality in order of causation, and this "beginning" is, therefore,

*I.e. the King James—*Ed.*
†"Fountain and origin"—*Ed.*

a *continuous* fact, *always* present and not to be conceived of as something which has been left behind and done with.

The same principle was, of course, the "beginning" of the entity in point of time also, however far back in the ages we may suppose it to have first evolved into separate existence, so that whether we apply the idea to the cosmos or to the individual, the words "in the beginning" both carry us back to the primordial out-push from nonmanifestation into manifestation, and also rivet our attention upon the same power as still at work as the causal principle both in ourselves and in everything else around us. In both these senses, then, the opening words of the Bible tell us that the "beginning" of everything is "God," or Spirit in the universal.

The next statement—that God created the heaven and the earth—brings us to the consideration of the Bible way of using words. The fact that the Bible deals with spiritual and psychic matters makes it of necessity an esoteric book, and therefore, in common with all other esoteric literature, it makes a symbolic use of words for the purpose of succinctly expressing ideas which would otherwise require elaborate explanation, and also for the purpose of concealing its meaning from those who are not yet safely to be entrusted with it. But this need not discourage the earnest student, for by comparing one part of the Bible with another he will find that the Bible itself affords the clue to the translation of its own symbolical vocabulary.

Here, as in so many other instances, the Master has given us the key to the right interpretation. He says that the Kingdom of Heaven is *within* us; in other words, that "Heaven" is the kingdom of the innermost and spiritual; and if so, then by necessary implication "Earth" must be the symbol of the opposite extreme and must metaphorically mean the outermost and material. We are starting the history of the evolution of the world in which we live; that is to say, this Power, which the Bible calls "God," is first presented to us in the opening words of Genesis at a stage immediately preceding the commencement of a stupendous work.

Now what are the conditions necessary for the doing of any work? Obviously there must be something that works and something that is worked upon—an active and a passive factor; an energy and a material on or in which that energy operates. This, then, is what is meant by the creation of Heaven and Earth; it is that operation of the eternally subsisting ONE upon Itself which produces its dual expression as Energy and Substance. And here remark carefully that this does not mean a *separation*, for Energy can only be exhibited by reason of something which is energized; or, in other words, for Life to manifest at all, there must be something that lives. This is an all-important truth, for our conception of ourselves as beings separate from the Divine Life is the root of all our troubles.

In its first verse, therefore, the Bible starts us with the conception of Energy or Life *inherent in substance* and shows us that the two constitute a dual-unity which is the first manifestation of the Infinite Unmanifested ONE; and if the reader will think these things out for himself, he will see that these are primary intuitions the contrary of which it is impossible to conceive. He may, if he please, introduce a Demiurge* as part of the machinery for the production of the world, but then he has to account for his Demiurge, which brings him back to the Undistributed ONE of which I speak, and its first manifestation as Energy-inherent-in-Substance; and if he is driven back to this position, then it becomes clear that his Demiurge is a totally unnecessary wheel in the train of evolutionary machinery. And the gratuitous introduction of a factor which does no work but what could equally be done without it is contrary to anything we can observe in Nature or can conceive of a Self-evolving Power.

But we are particularly cautioned against the

*A "subordinate deity" who creates the material world—*Ed.*

mistake of supposing that Substance is the same thing as Form, for we are told that the "earth was without form." This is important because it is just here that a very prolific source of error in metaphysical studies creeps in. We see Forms which, simply as masses, are devoid of an organized life corresponding to the particular form, and therefore we deny the inherency of Energy or Life in ultimate substance itself. As well deny the pungency of pepper because it is not in the particular pepper-pot we are accustomed to.

No, that primordial state of Substance with which the opening verse of the Bible is concerned is something very far removed from any conception we can have of Matter as formed into atoms or electrons. We are here only at the first stage of Involution, and the presence of material atoms is a stage, and by no means the earliest, in the process of Evolution.

We are next told that the Spirit of God moved upon the face of the waters. Here we have two factors, "Spirit" and "Water," and the initial movement is attributed to Spirit. This verse introduces us to that particular mode of manifestation of the Universal Substance which we may denominate the Psychic. This psychic mode of the Universal Substance may best be described as Cosmic Soul-

Essence—not, indeed, universal in the strictest sense otherwise than as always included in the original Primordial Essence, but universal to the particular world-system under formation, and as yet undifferentiated into any individual forms.

This is what the mediaeval writers spoke of as "the Soul of the Universe," or *Anima Mundi*, as distinguished from the Divine Self, or *Animus Dei*, and it is the universal psychic medium in which the nuclei of the forms hereafter to become consolidated on the plane of the concrete and material take their inception in obedience to the movement of the Spirit, or Thought. This is the realm of *Potential* Forms, and is the connecting link between Spirit, or pure Thought, and Matter, or concrete Form, and as such plays a most important part in the constitution of the Cosmos and of Man.

In our reading of the Bible as well as in our practical application of Mental Science, the existence of this intermediary between Spirit and Matter must never be lost sight of. We may call it the Distributive Medium, in passing through which the hitherto undistributed Energy of Spirit receives differentiation of direction and so ultimately produces differentiation of forms and relations on the outermost or visible plane. This is the Cosmic Element which is esoterically called "Water," and so long ago as the reign of Henry VIII, Dean Colet* explains it thus in a letter to his friend Randulph.

Dean Colet was very far from being a visionary. He was one of the precursors of the Reformation in England, and among the first to establish the study of Greek at Oxford; and as the founder of St. Paul's School in London, he took a leading part in introducing the system of public-school education† which is still in operation in this country. There is no mistaking Dean Colet for any other than a thoroughly level-headed and practical man, and his opinion as to the meaning of the word "Water" in this connection therefore carries great weight.

But we have the utterance of a yet higher authority on this subject, for the Master Himself concentrates His whole instruction to Nicodemus on the point that the New Birth results from the interaction of "Spirit" and "Water," especially emphasizing the fact that "the flesh" has no share in the operation. This distinction between "the flesh," or the outermost principle, and "Water" should be carefully noted. The emphasis laid by the Master on the nothingness of "the flesh" and the essentialness of "Water" must mark a distinction of

*John Colet (1466?–1519), English theologian and scholar —*Ed.*

†This largely corresponds to what in the United States would be called private-school education. —*Ed.*

the most important kind, and we shall find it very helpful in unravelling the meaning of many passages of the Bible to grasp this distinction at the outset.

The action of "Spirit" upon "Water" is that of an active upon a passive principle; and the result of any sort of Work is to reconstruct the material worked upon into a form which it did not possess before. Now the new form to be produced, whatever it may be, is a *result* and therefore is not to be enumerated among the causes of its own production.

Hence it is a self-obvious truism that any act of creative power must take place at a more interior level than that of the form to be created; and accordingly, whether in the Old or the New Testament, the creative action is always contemplated as taking place between the Spirit and the Water, whether we are thinking of producing a new world or a new man. We must always go back to First Cause operating on Primary Substance.

We are told that the first product of the movement of Spirit upon Water was Light, thereby suggesting an analogy with the discoveries of modern science that light and heat are modes of motion. But the statement that the Sun was not created till the fourth day guards us against the mistake of supposing that what is here meant is the light visible to the physical eye. Rather, it is that All-pervading Inner Light, of which I shall have more to say by and by, and which only becomes visible as the corresponding sense of inward vision begins to be developed; it is that psychic condition of the Universal Substance in which the auras of the *potentials* of all forms may be discovered, and where, consciously or unconsciously, the Spirit determines the forms of those things which are to be.

Like all other knowledge, the knowledge of the Inner Light is capable of application at higher and at lower levels, and the premature recognition of its power at the lower levels, uncontrolled by the recognition of its higher phases, is one of the most dangerous acquisitions; but duly regulated by the higher knowledge, the lower is both safe and legitimate, for in its due order it also is part of the Universal Harmony.

The initial Light having thus been produced, the introduction of the firmament on the second day indicates the separation of the spiritual principles of the different members of the world-system from one another, and the third day sees the emanation of Earth from "the Water," or the production of the actual corporeal system of Nature—the commencement of the process of Evolution. Up to this point the action has been entirely upon the inner plane of "Water"—that is to say, a process of

Involution—and consistently with this it was impossible for the heavenly bodies to begin giving physical light until the fourth day, for until then no physical sun or planets could have existed.

With the fourth day, however, the physical universe is differentiated into shape; and on the fifth day the *terrestrial* waters begin to take their share in the evolutionary process, by spontaneously producing fish and fowl. And here we may remark in passing how Genesis has forestalled modern science in the discovery that birds are anatomically more closely related to fishes than to land animals. The terrestrial earth (I call it so to distinguish it from symbolic "earth"), already on the third day impregnated with the vegetable principle, takes up the evolutionary work on the sixth day, producing all those other animal races which had not already originated in the waters, and thus the preparation of the world as an abode for Man is completed.

It would be difficult to give a more concise statement of Evolution. Originating Spirit subsists at first as simple Unity, then it differentiates itself into the active and passive principles spoken of as "Heaven" and "Earth," or "Spirit" and "Water." From these proceed Light and the separation into their respective spheres of the spiritual principles of the different planets, each carrying with it the potential of the self-reproducing power.

Then we pass into the realm of realization, and the work that has been done on the interior planes is now reproduced in physical manifestation, thus marking a still further unfoldment; and finally, in the phrases "let the waters bring forth" and "let the earth bring forth," the land and water of our habitable globe are distinctly stated to be the sources from which all vegetable and animal forms have been evolved. Thus creation is described as the self-transforming action of the ONE unanalysable Spirit passing by successive transitions into all the varieties of manifestations that fill the universe.

And here we may notice a point which has puzzled commentators unacquainted with the principles on which the Bible is written. This is the expression "the evening and the morning were the first, second, etc., day." Why, it is asked, does each day begin with the evening? and various attempts have been made to explain it in accordance with Jewish methods of reckoning time. But as soon as we see what the Bible statement of creation is, the reason at once becomes clear. The second verse of the Bible tells us that the starting-point was Darkness, and the coming forth of Light out of Darkness cannot be stated in any other order than the dawning of morning from night.

It is the dawning into manifestation out of non-manifestation, and this happens at each successive stage of the evolutionary process. We should notice, also, that nothing is said as to the remainder of each day. All that we hear of each day is as "the morning," thus indicating the grand truth that when once a Divine day opens, it never again descends into the shades of night. It is always "morning."

The Spiritual Sun is always climbing higher and higher, but never passes the zenith or commences to decline—a truth which Swedenborg expresses by saying that the Spiritual Sun is always seen in the eastern heavens at an angle of forty-five degrees above the horizon. What a glorious and inspiring truth: when once God begins a work, that work will never cease, but will go on forever expanding into more and more radiant forms of strength and beauty, because it is the expression of the Infinite, which is Itself Love, Wisdom, and Power.

These days of creation are still in their prime and forever will be so, and the germs of the New Heavens and the New Earth which the Bible promises are already maturing in the heavens and earth that now are, waiting only, as St. Paul tells us, for the manifestation of the Sons of God to follow up the old principle of Evolution to still further expansion in the glory that shall be revealed.

As himself included in the great Whole, Man is no exception to the Universal Law of Evolution. It has often been remarked that the account of his creation is twofold, the two statements being contained in the first and second chapters of Genesis respectively. But this is precisely in accordance with the method adopted regarding the rest of creation.

First we are told of the creation in the realm of the invisible and psychic—that is to say, the process of Involution; and afterwards we are told of the creation on the plane of the concrete and material—that is to say, the process of Evolution. And since Involution is the cause and Evolution the effect, the Bible observes this order both in the account of the creation of the world and in that of the creation of Man.

In regard to his physical structure, Man's body, we are told, is formed from the "earth"—that is, by a combination of the same material elements as all other concrete forms; and thus in the physical Man, the evolutionary process attains its culmination in the production of a material vehicle capable of serving as the starting-point for a further advance, which has now to be made on the plane of the Intellectual and Spiritual.

The principle of Evolution is never departed from, but its further action now includes the intelligent cooperation of the evolving Individuality itself as a necessary factor in the work. The development of merely animal Man is the spontaneous operation of Nature, but the development of the mental Man can only result from his own recognition of the Law of the Self-expression of Spirit as operating in himself.

It is, therefore, for the setting forth of Man's power to *use* this Law that the Bible was written; and accordingly, the great fact on which it seeks to rivet our attention in its first utterance regarding Man is that he is made in the image and likeness of God. A very little reflection will show us that this likeness cannot be in the outward form, for the Universal Spirit in which all things subsist cannot be limited by shape. It is a Principle permeating all things as their innermost substance and vivifying energy, and of it the Bible tells us that "in the beginning" there was nothing else.

Now the one and only conception we can have of this Universal Life-Principle is that of Creative Power producing infinitely varied expressions of itself by Thought, for we cannot ascribe any other initial mode of movement to Spirit but that of thought—although as taking place in the Universal, this mode of Thought must necessarily be, relatively to the individual and particular, a subconscious activity. The likeness, therefore, between God and Man must be a mental likeness, and since the only fact which, up to this point, the Bible has told us regarding the Universal Mind is its Creative

Power, the resemblance indicated can only consist in the reproduction of the same Creative Power in the Mind of Man.

As we progress, we shall find that the whole Bible turns on this one fundamental fact. The Creative Power is inherent in our Thought, and we can by no means divest ourselves of it; but because we are ignorant that we possess this power, or because we misapprehend the conditions for its beneficial employment, we need much instruction in the nature of our own as yet unrecognized possibilities; and it is the purpose of the Bible to give us this teaching.

A little consideration of the terms of the evolutionary process will show us that since there is no other source from which it can proceed, the Individual Mind, which is the essential entity that we call Man, can be no other than a concentration of the Universal Mind into individual consciousness. Man's Mind is, therefore, a miniature reproduction of the Divine Mind, just as fire has always the same igneous qualities whether the centre of combustion be large or small; and so it is on *this* fact that the Bible would fix our attention from first to last, knowing that if the interior realm of Causation be maintained in a harmonious order, the external realm of Effects is certain to exhibit corresponding health, happiness, and beauty.

And further, if the human mind is the exact

image and likeness of the Divine, then its creative power must be equally unlimited. Its *mode* is different, being directed to the individual and particular, but its *quality* is the same; and this becomes evident if we reflect that it is not possible to set any limit to Thought, and that its only limitations are such as are set by the limited conceptions of the individual who thinks. And it is precisely here that the difficulty comes in. Our Thought must necessarily be limited by our conceptions. We cannot think of something which we cannot conceive; and therefore, the more limited our conceptions, the more limited will be our thought, and its creations will accordingly be limited in a corresponding degree.

It is for this reason that the ultimate purpose of all true instruction is to lead us into that Divine Light where we shall see things beyond the range of any past experiences—things which have not entered into the heart of man to conceive, revealings of the Divine Spirit opening to us untold worlds of splendour, delight, and unending achievement. But in our earlier stages of development, where we are still surrounded by the mists of ignorance, this correspondence between the range of Thought's creations and the range of our conceptions brings about the catastrophe of "the Fall," which forms the subject of our next chapter.

CHAPTER 2

The Fall

In the last chapter we reached the conclusion that in the nature of things, Thought must always be limited by the range of the intelligence which gives rise to it. The power of Thought as the creative agent is perfectly unlimited in itself, but its action is limited by the particular conception which it is sent forth to embody. If it is a wide conception based upon an enlarged perception of truth, the thought which dwells upon it will produce corresponding conditions. This is self-evident; it is simply the statement that an instrument will not do work to which the hand of the workman does not apply it; and if the student will only fix this very simple idea in his mind, he will find in it the key to the whole mystery of man's power of self-evolution. Let us make our first use of this key to unlock the mystery of the story of Eden.

It is hardly necessary to say that the story of Eden

is an allegory: that is clearly shown by the nature of the two trees that grew in the centre of the garden—the Tree of the Knowledge of Good and Evil and the Tree of Life. This allegory is one repeated in many lands and ages, as in the classical fable of the Garden of the Hesperides and in the mediaeval Romance of the Rose; always the idea is repeated of a garden in whose centre grows some life-giving fruit or flower which is the reward of him who discovers the secret by which the centre of the garden may be reached.

The meaning in all these stories is the same. The garden is the Garden of the Soul, and the Tree of Life is that innermost perception of Spirit of which the Master said that it would be a well of water springing up to everlasting life to all who realized it. It is the garden which elsewhere in Scripture is called "the garden of the Lord"; and in accordance with the nature of the garden, the plants which grow in it—and which man has to tend and cultivate—are thoughts and ideas; and the chief of them are his idea of Life and his idea of Knowledge, and these occupy the centre of the garden because all our other ideas must take their colour from them.

We must recollect that human life is a drama whose action takes place in three worlds, and therefore, in reading the Bible, we must always make sure which world we are at any moment reading about—the spiritual, the intellectual, or the physical. In the spiritual world, which is that of the supreme ideal, there exists nothing but the potential of the absolutely perfect; and it is on this account that in the opening chapter of the Bible we read that God saw that all his work was good—the Divine eye could find no flaw anywhere; and we should note carefully that this absolutely good creation included Man also.

But as soon as we descend to the Intellectual world, which is the world of man's *conception* of things, it is quite different; and until man comes to realize the truly spiritual, and therefore perfectly good, essential nature of all things, there is room for any amount of *mis*-conception, resulting in a corresponding misdirection of man's creative instrument of Thought, which thus produces correspondingly misinformed realities.

Now the perfect life of Adam and Eve in Eden is the picture of Man as he exists in the spiritual world. It is not the tradition of some bygone age, but a symbolical representation of what we all *are* in our *innermost* being, thus recalling the words of the Master recorded in the Gospel of the Egyptians. He was asked when the Kingdom of Heaven should come and replied, "When that which is without shall be as that which is within"* —in other words, when the perfection of the innermost spiritual essence shall be reproduced in the external part. In the story of Man's pristine life of innocence and joy in Paradise, we are reading on the level of the highest of the three worlds.

The story of "the Fall" brings us to the envelopment of this spiritual nature in the lower intellectual and material natures, through which alone it can obtain perfect individualization and Man become a reality instead of remaining only a Divine dream. In the allegory, Man is warned by God that Death will be the consequence of eating the fruit of the tree of the Knowledge of Good and Evil. This is not the threat of a sentence to be passed by God, but a warning as to the nature of the fruit itself; but this warning is disregarded by Eve, and she shares the forbidden fruit with Adam, and they are both expelled from Eden and become subject to Death as the consequence.

Now if Eden is the garden of the Soul, it is clear that Adam and Eve cannot be separate personages, but must be two principles in the human individuality which are so closely united as to be represented

*See The Gospel of Thomas 37:27 in *The Nag Hammadi Library*, James Robinson, ed. (San Francisco: Harper, 1978/88), p. 129. —*Ed.*

by a wedded pair. What, then, are these principles? St. Paul makes a very remarkable statement regarding Adam and Eve. He tells us that "Adam was not deceived, but the woman being deceived was in the transgression" (1 Tim. 2:14). We have, therefore, Bible warrant for saying that Adam was not deceived; but at the same time, the story of the Fall clearly shows that he was expelled from Eden for partaking of the fruit at Eve's instigation.

To satisfy both statements, therefore, we require to find in Adam and Eve two principles, one of which is capable of being deceived, and is deceived, and falls in consequence of the deception; and the other of which is incapable of being deceived but yet is involved with the fall of the former. This is the problem which has to be worked out, and the names of Adam and Eve supply the solution.

Eve, we are told, was so called because she was the mother of all living (Gen. 3:20). Eve, then, is the Mother of Life, a subject to which I shall have to refer again by and by. *Eve*, both syllables being pronounced, is the same word which in some Oriental languages is written "Hawa," by which name she is called in the Koran, and signifies Breath—the principle which we are told in Genesis 2:7 constitutes Man a living Soul.

Adam is rendered in the margin of the Bible "earth," or "red earth," and according to another derivation the name may also be rendered as "Not-breath." And thus in these two names we have the description of two principles, one of which is "Breath" and Life-conveying, while the other is "Not-breath" and is nothing but earth.

It requires no great skill to recognize in these the Soul and the Body. Then St. Paul's meaning becomes clear. Any work on physiology will tell you that the human body is made up of certain chemical materials—so much chalk, so much carbon, so much water, etc., etc. Obviously these substances cannot be deceived, because they have no intelligence, and any deception that occurs must be accepted by the soul or intellectual principle, which is Eve, the mother of the individual life.

New Thought readers will have no difficulty in following the meaning of the poet Spenser when he says:

> For the soul of the body form doth take,
> For soul is form and doth the body make.

and since the soul is "the builder of the body," the deception which causes wrong thinking on the part of the intellectual man reproduces itself in physical imperfection and in adverse external circumstances.

What, then, is the deception which causes the

"Fall"? This is figured by the Serpent. The serpent is a very favourite emblem in all ancient esoteric literature and symbolism and is sometimes used in a positive and sometimes in a negative sense. In either case it means life—not the Originating Life-Principle, but the ultimate outcome of that Life-Principle in its most external form of manifestation. This, of course, is not bad in itself. Recognized in full realization of the fact that it comes from God, it is the completion of the Divine work by outward manifestation; and in this sense it becomes the serpent which Moses lifted up in the wilderness.

But without the recognition of it as the ultimate mode of the Divine Spirit (which is *all* that is), it becomes the deadly reptile, not lifted up, but crawling flat upon the ground. It is that ignorant conception of things which cannot see the spiritual element in them and therefore attributes all their energy of action and reaction to *themselves*, not perceiving that they are the creations of a higher power.

Ignorant of the Divine Law of Creation, we do not look beyond secondary causes; and therefore because our own creative thought-power is ever externalizing conditions *representative of our conceptions*, we necessarily become more and more involved in the meshes of a network of circumstances from which we can find no way of escape. How these circumstances come about we cannot tell. We may call it blind chance, or iron destiny, or inscrutable Providence, but because we are ignorant of the true Law of Primary Causation, we never suspect the real fact, which is that the originating power of all this inharmony is ourself.

This is the great deception. We believe the serpent, or that conception of life which sees nothing beyond secondary causation, and consequently we accept the Knowledge of Evil as being equally necessary with the Knowledge of Good; and so we eat of the tree of the Knowledge of Good *and* of Evil. It is this dual aspect of knowledge that is deadly, but knowledge itself is nowhere condemned in Scripture; on the contrary, it is repeatedly stated to be the foundation of all progress. "Wisdom is a Tree of Life to them that lay hold upon her," says the Book of Proverbs; "Salvation is of the Jews because we *know* what we worship," says Jesus; and so on throughout the Bible.

But what *is* deadly to the soul of Man is the conception that Evil is a subject of Knowledge as well as Good—for this reason: that by thinking of Evil as a subject to be studied, we thereby attribute to it a substantive existence of its own; in other words, we look upon it as something having a self-originating power, which, as we advance in our studies, we shall find more and more clearly is not the case. And so, by the Law of the creative working of Thought, we bring the Evil into existence. We have not yet penetrated the great secret of the difference between causes and conditions.*

But this knowledge of our thought-action is not reached in the earlier history of the race or of the individual, for the simple reason that all evolution takes place by Growth; and consequently the history of Adam and Eve *in realization*—that is, the external life of humanity as distinguished from our simultaneous existence on the supreme plane of Spirit—commences with their expulsion from Eden and their conflict with a world of sorrows and difficulties.

If the reader realizes how this expulsion results from the soul accepting Evil as a subject of Knowledge, he will now be able to understand certain further facts. We are told that "the Lord God said, 'Behold the man is become as one of us to know good and evil'; and now lest he put forth his hand and take of the tree of life and eat and live for ever; the Lord God sent him forth from the Garden of Eden" (Gen. 3:22,23). Looked at superficially, this seems like jealousy that Man should have attained the same knowledge as God, and fear lest he

*See my *Edinburgh Lectures on Mental Science*.

should take the further step that would make him altogether God's equal. But such a reading of the text is babyish and indicates no conception of God as Universal All-originating Spirit, and we must therefore look for some deeper interpretation.

The First Commandment is the recognition of the Divine Unity, a fact on which Jesus laid special emphasis when he was asked which was the chief commandment of the Law; and the purpose is to guard us against the root-error from which all other forms of error spring. If the mathematical statement of Truth is that God is ONE, then the mathematical expression of error is that God is Zero, and as the latter position has sometimes been taken by teachers of reputation, it may be well to show the student where the fallacy lies.

The conclusion that the mathematical expression of God is Zero is reached in this way: as soon as you can conceive of anything as *being*, you can also conceive of it as *not-being*; in other words, the conception of any positive implies also the conception of its corresponding negative. Consequently, the conception of the positive or of the negative by itself is only half the conception, and a whole conception implies the recognition of both.

Therefore, since God contains the all, He must contain the negative as well as the positive of all potentiality, and the equal balance of positive and negative is Zero. But the radical error of this argument is the assumption that it is possible for two principles to neutralize each other, one of which *is*, and the other of which *is not*.

We find the principle of neutralization by means of equilibration throughout Nature, but the equilibration is always between two things each of which actually exists. Thus in chemistry we find an acid exactly equilibrating an alkali and producing a neutral substance which is neither acid nor alkali; but this is because the acid and the alkali both really exist; each of them is something that *is*. But what should we say to a chemical formula which required us to produce a neutral substance by equilibrating an acid which did exist by an alkali which did not? Yet this is precisely the sort of equilibration we are asked to accept by those who would make Zero the mathematical expression of All-originating Being. They say that a Universal Principle which *is* is exactly balanced by a Universal Principle which *is not*; they affirm that Nothing is the equivalent of Something.

This is mere juggling with words and figures, and wilfully shutting our eyes to the fact that the only quality of Nothing is Nothingness. Can anything be plainer than the old philosophic dictum *ex nihilo nihil fit* ("nothing is made out of nothing")—? Disintegrating forces there are in Nature, but they do not proceed out of Nothing. They are the ONE positive power acting at lower levels—not the absence of the One Universal Energy but that same Energy working with less complex concentration and specific purpose than when directed by those higher modes *of itself* which constitute individual intelligences.

There is no such thing as a Negative Power, in the sense of power which is not the ONE All-originating Power. All energy is *some* mode of manifestation of the ONE, and it is *always making* something, though in doing so it may unmake something else; and what we loosely speak of as negative forces are the operation of the cosmical Law of Transition from one Form to another.

Above this there is a higher Law, to lead us to the realization of which is the whole object of the Bible, and that is the Law of Individual Selection. It does not do away with the Law of Transition, for without transition there could be no Evolution, and the glory of Eternal Life is in continuous Evolution; but it substitutes the Individual Law of *conscious* Life for the Impersonal Cosmic Law, and effects transition by *living* processes of assimilation and readjustment which more perfectly build up the individuality, instead of by a process of unbalanced disintegration which would destroy it. This is the Living Law of Liberty, which at every stage of its progress makes us not less, but more and yet more, *ourselves.*

It is for this reason that the Bible so strongly insists upon the mathematical statement that God is ONE, and in fact makes this the basis of all that it has to say. God is Life, Expression, Reality; and how can these things comport with Nothingness? All we can know of any invisible power is through the effects we see it produce. Of electricity and chemical attraction it may be truly said that "no man hath seen them or can see them"; yet we know them by their working, and we rightly argue that if they work, they exist. The same argument applies to the Divine Spirit. It is that which *is* and not that which *is not*; and therefore I ask the student who would realize reality and not nothingness once for all to convince himself of the fallaciousness of the argument that the Divine Being is Not-being, or that Naught is the same thing as ONE.

If he starts his search for Reality by assuming what contradicts mathematics and common sense, he can never expect to find Reality, for he has denied its existence at the very outset and carries that initial denial all the way along with him. But if he realizes that all relations, whether *relatively* positive or negative, must necessarily be relations between factors which actually exist, and that there can be no relation with nothing, then, because he has assumed Reality in his premises, he will eventually find it in his conclusions and will learn that the Great Reality is the ONE expressing itself as the MANY, and the MANY recognizing themselves in the ONE.

The more advanced student will have no difficulty in recognizing the particular schools of teaching to which these remarks apply; their mathematics are unassailable, but the assumptions on which they make their selection of terms in the first instance are totally inapplicable to the subject-matter to which they apply them, for that subject is *Life-in-itself*.

Now the deception into which Eve falls is mathematically represented by saying that God = Zero, and thus attributing to Evil the same self-existence as to Good. There is no such thing as Absolute Evil; and what we recognize as Evil is the ONE Good Power working as Disintegrating Force, because we have not yet learnt to direct it in such a way that it shall perform the functions of transition to higher degrees of Life without any disintegration of our individuality either in person or circumstances. It is this disintegrating action that makes the ONE Power *appear* evil relatively to ourselves; and, so long as we conceive ourselves thus related to it, it does look as though it were Zero balancing in itself the two opposite forces of Life and Death, Good and Evil, and it is in this sense that "God" is said to know both.

But this is a conception very different to that of the All-productive ONE, and arises, not from the true nature of Being, but from our own confused Thought. But because the action of our Thought is always creative, the mere fact of our regarding Evil as an affirmative force in itself makes it so *relatively to ourselves*; and therefore no sooner do we fear evil than we begin to create the evil that we fear. To extinguish evil, we must learn not to fear it, and that means to cease recognizing it as having any power of its own; and so our salvation comes from realizing that in truth there is nothing but the good.

But this knowledge can only be attained through long experience, which will at last bring Man to the place where he is able to deduce Truth from *a priori* principles* and to learn that his past experiences of evil have proceeded from his own inverted conceptions and are not founded upon Truth but upon its opposite. If, then, it were possible for him to attain the knowledge which would enable him to live forever before gaining this experience, the result would be an immortality of misery, and therefore the Law of Nature renders it

*Principles derived from self-evident propositions—*Ed.*

impossible for him to reach the knowledge which would place immortality within his grasp until he has gained that deep insight into the true working of causation which is necessary to make Eternal Life a prize worth having. For these reasons, Man is represented as being expelled from Eden lest he should eat of the Tree of Life and live forever.

Before quitting this subject we must glance briefly at the sentences pronounced upon the man, the woman, and the serpent. The serpent, in this connection being the principle of error, which results in Death, can never come into any sort of reconciliation with the Divine Spirit, which is Truth and Life, and therefore the only possible pronouncement upon the serpent is a curse—that is, a sentence of destruction; and the Bible goes on to show the stages by which this destruction is ultimately worked out. The penalty to Adam, or the corporeal body, is that of having to earn his bread by the sweat of his brow—that is, by toilsome labor, which would not be necessary if the true law of the creative exercise of our Thought were understood. The woman passes under a painful physiological law, but at the same time final deliverance and restoration from the "Fall" is promised through her instrumentality: her seed shall crush the serpent's head—that is, shall utterly destroy that false principle which the serpent represents.

Since the Woman is the Soul, or Individual Mind, her progeny must be *thoughts* and *ideas*. New ideas are not brought forth easily; they are the result of painful experiences and of long mental labor; and thus the physiological analogy contained in the text exactly illustrates the birth of new ideas into the world. And as the evolution of the Soul proceeds toward higher and higher intelligence, there is a corresponding increase in the lifeward tendency of its ideas, and thus there is enmity between the seed of "the Woman," or the enlightened conception of the principles of Life, and the seed of "the Serpent," or the opposite and unenlightened conception.

This is the same warfare which we find in Revelation between "the Woman" and "the Dragon." But in the end the victory remains with "the Woman" and her "Seed." During the progress of the struggle, the Serpent must bruise the heel of the Divine Seed—that is to say, must impede and retard the progress of Truth on the earth; but Truth must conquer at last and crush the Serpent's head so that it shall never rise up again forever. The "Seed of the Woman"—the Fruit of the spiritually enlightened Mind, which must at last achieve the final victory—is that supreme ideal which is the recognition of Man's Divine Sonship. It is the realization of the fact that he is, indeed, the image and likeness of God. This is the Truth the knowledge of which Jesus said would set us free, and each one who attains to this knowledge realizes that he is at once the Son of Man and the Son of God.

Thus the story of the Fall contains also the statement of the principle of the Rising-again. It is the history of the human race, because it is first the history of the individual soul, and to each one of us the ancient wisdom says, *"de te fabula narratur."** These opening chapters of Genesis are, therefore, an epitome of all that the Bible afterwards unfolds in fuller detail, and the whole may be summed up in the following terms:

The great Truth concerning Man is that he is the image and likeness of God.

Man is at first ignorant of this Truth, and this ignorance is his Fall.

Man at last comes to the perfect knowledge of this Truth, and this knowledge is his Rising-again; and these principles will expand until they bring us to the full Expression of the Life that is in us in all the glories of the Heavenly Jerusalem.

*Loosely, "It is *you* that the story is about"—*Ed.*

CHAPTER 3

Israel

The space at my disposal will allow me only to touch upon a few of the most conspicuous points in that portion of the Bible narrative which takes us from the story of Eden to the Mission of Moses, for the reader will kindly bear in mind that I am not writing a commentary on the whole Bible, but only a brief introduction to its study.

The episode of Cain and Abel will be dealt with in the next chapter, and I will therefore pass on at once to the Deluge. As most of my readers probably know, this story is not confined to the Jewish and Christian Scriptures, but is met with in one form or another in all the most ancient traditions of the world, and this universal consensus of mankind leaves no doubt of the occurrence of some overwhelming cataclysm which has indelibly stamped itself upon the memory of all nations.

Whether science will ever succeed in working out the problem of its extent and of the physical conditions that gave rise to it, remains to be seen, but it does not appear unreasonable to associate it with the tradition handed down to us by Plato of the sinking of the great continent of Atlantis, which is said to have once occupied the area now covered by the Atlantic ocean. I am well aware that some geologists dispute the possibility of any radical changes having ever taken place in the distribution of the land and water surfaces of the globe, but there are at least equally good opinions on the other side, and if there is any fact in the world's history regarding which tradition is unanimous, it is the catastrophe of the Deluge.

And here I would draw attention to the fact that the Bible specially warns us against the opinion that no such catastrophe ever took place, and points out this opinion as one of the signs of the time of the end, speaking of it as determined ignorance, and telling us that a similar catastrophe, only by fire instead of water, will at some future period overwhelm the existing world (2 Peter 3); and I would add that the possible conditions for such an event may not unreasonably be inferred from certain facts in the science of astronomy. It is not my present purpose, however, to enter into the scientific and historical aspects of the Deluge tradition, but to point out its significance in that *inner* meaning of the Bible which I wish the student to grasp.

In the story as handed down by all nations, the Deluge is attributed to the wickedness of mankind, and according to some very ancient traditions this wickedness took largely the form of sorcery—a word which may perhaps provoke a smile in the uninitiated reader, but which holds a conspicuous place in the list of those causes which in the Book of Revelation are enumerated as leading to exclusion from the Heavenly City; and it will become sufficiently clear why it should do so when we learn what it really means. Coupling this tradition with the symbolical significance of "water," a deluge would indicate a total submergence in a psychic environment which had become too powerful to be held under control.

The psychic world is an integral part of the universe, and the psychic element is an integral part of man; and it is in this circulus that we find the plastic material which forms the nucleus for those attractions which eventually consolidate as external facts. The psychic realm is therefore the realm of tremendous potentialities, and the deeper our knowledge of its laws, the greater we see to be the need for bringing these potentialities under a higher control.

Now the opening verses of Genesis have shown us that "water" without the movement of the Spirit is darkness and the abode of chaos. The movement of the Spirit is the only power that can control the turbulence of "the waters" and bring them into that harmonious action which will result in forms of

Life, Beauty, and Peace; and in the world of Man's Mind this movement of the Spirit upon "the waters" takes place exactly in proportion as the individual recognizes the true nature of the Divine Spirit and wills to reflect its image and likeness.

Where this recognition takes place, the psychic forces are brought under the control of a harmonizing power which, reflecting itself into them, can only produce that which is Good and Beautiful, on a small scale at first because of our infantine knowledge of the powers with which we are dealing, but continually growing with our growth until the whole psychic world opens out before us as a limitless realm filled with the Glory of God and the Love of Man and the shapes of beauty to which these give rise.

But if a man forces his way into that realm on no other basis than his individual strength of will, he does so without reckoning that his will is itself a product of the psychic plane, and only one among untold organized entities and unorganized forces which sooner or later will overpower him and hurry him to age-long destruction—"age-long," for I use the Bible word *aionios*, which, as the learned Farrar* has shown in his *Eternal Hope*, does not mean absolutely endless; yet, if we reflect what may

*Frederic William Farrar (1831–1903), English clergyman and writer—*Ed.*

be included in this word—infinite periods, perhaps, of withdrawal and renewal of our whole planetary system—we may well stand aghast at such prodigious ruin.

But if such dangers are in it, may we not say that we will have nothing to do with the psychic realm? No, for by our nature we are always immersed in it: it is *within* us, and we are, and always must be, inhabitants of it, and we are always unconsciously using its forces and being reacted upon by them. What we need, therefore, is not to escape from what is an essential part of our nature, but to learn to vivify this otherwise dark realm with the warmth of Divine Love and the illumination of Divine Light.

But the Bible tells how very far the antediluvian* world was from recognizing these Divine principles, for "the earth was filled with violence," and, except in the family of Noah, the true worship of God had ceased among men. And remark this word "violence" as the summing-up of human iniquity. Violence is the clashing of individual wills not harmonized by the recognition of any *unifying* principle. The ONE-ness of the Spirit from which all individualization proceeds is entirely lost sight of, and "each for himself" becomes the ruling prin-

*Prior to the flood described in Genesis—*Ed.*

ciple—a principle which cannot but result in violence under whatever disguise it may be masked for a time.

The earth filled with violence was the outward correspondence of the inward mental state of the masses of mankind, and we may, therefore, well imagine what the nature of their operations in the symbolic world of "Water" must have been. This state of things had been growing for generations until at last the inevitable result arrived, and the moral deluge produced its correspondence in the physical world.

The uninstructed reader will doubtless smile at my reference to a psychic environment, but those who have obtained at least some glimpses beyond the threshold will see the force of my argument when I direct their attention to the signs of a recurrence of a similar state of things at the present day. Research in various directions is making clearer and clearer the reality of the psychic forces, and increasing numbers are beginning to get some measure of practical insight into them; and while I rejoice to say that we see these opening powers being employed for the most part under the direction of sincere religious feeling and with charitable intention, yet there are not wanting reports of opposite uses, and this in connection with specific localities where the inverted employment of these great powers is secretly practised according to methodized system.

I cannot too strongly warn the student against any connection with such societies,* and their existence is a terrible comment upon the Master's description of the latter days, which, He expressly tells us, will reproduce the character of those which immediately preceded the flood. The sole safeguard is in recognizing the Divine Spirit as the only Source of Power, and in regarding every action, whether of thought, word, or deed, as being in its form and measure an act of Divine worship. This is what St. Paul means when he says "Pray without ceasing." What needs to be cultivated is the habitual mental attitude that leads us to see God in *all* things, and it is for this reason that the foundation of conscious spiritual Life is that First Commandment to the consideration of which we are approaching.

It was, therefore, in consequence of their entire denial of the Divine Spirit that the antediluvians raised up an adverse power which at last became too strong for them to control. And here let me once for all set the student right with regard to

*I.e. those that practice "left-handed" occultism, or "black magic." See "The Perversion of Truth," in *Collected Essays of Thomas Troward*, pp. 95–107. A relevant book-length treatment is *Psychic Self-Defense*, by Dion Fortune.—*Ed.*

those passages of the Bible in which God is represented as making up His mind to inflict injury, as in the announcement of the impending Deluge. These expressions are figurative. They represent the entrance upon the scene of that Cosmic Law of Disintegration which necessarily comes into play as soon as the highest directing power of Intelligence is inhibited; and therefore as soon as a man wilfully thrusts from himself the recognition of the Universal Spirit in its higher manifestations as the Guardian and the Guide, he ipso facto calls it into action in its lower manifestations as the Universal Cosmic Force.

The reason for this will appear more clearly from a careful study of the relations between the Personal and the Impersonal modes of Spirit, but the explanation of these relations would occupy too large a space to be entered upon here, and the reader must be referred to other works on the subject. In the present connection it is sufficient to say that we can never get rid of God, for we ourselves are manifestations of His Being, and if we will not have *Him* as the Good, we shall be compelled to accept *It* as the Evil. This is what the Master meant when He said in the parable that on the lord's return to his city, he ordered those who would not accept him to reign over them to be slain before him.

Noah and his three sons are rescued from the universal overthrow by means of the Ark. As I am concerned in the present book with the inner meaning of the Bible rather than with the historical facts, I must leave the reader to form his own conclusions regarding the literal measurements of that vessel; but I would take this opportunity of observing that where distinct numbers and measurements are given in the Bible, they are not introduced at haphazard. From the standpoint of ordinary arithmetic they may seem to be so, and the main argument of Bishop Colenso's great work on the Pentateuch* is based on these apparent discrepancies. For instance, speaking of the sacrifices to be offered for women after childbirth, he points out that during the march through the desert these could, according to the text, only be offered by Aaron and his two sons, and that calculated on ordinary averages, the offering of these sacrifices would have occupied each of these three priests fourteen hours a day without one moment's rest or intermission (vol. 1, p. 123). From the point of view of simple arithmetic this result is unavoidable; but I cannot endorse the Bishop's conclusion that the scribes who wrote the Pentateuch under the

*John William Colenso (1814–1883), *The Pentateuch and Book of Joshua Critically Examined* (London, 1870)—*Ed.*

direction of Ezra introduced any numbers that occurred to them without considering how they would work out.

On the contrary, such investigation as I have been able to make into the subject convinces me that the Bible numbers are calculated with the most rigid accuracy, and with the very deepest thought of the results to which they will work out —only this is done according to a certain symbolic system known as Sacred Numeration; and the very impracticability of the figures when tested by ordinary arithmetic is intended to put us upon enquiry for some deeper meaning below the surface. To explain the principles of Sacred Numeration would be beyond the scope of an elementary book like the present, and probably few readers would care to undertake the requisite amount of study; but we must not suppose that the numbers given in the Bible are without significance whenever ordinary methods of calculation fail to elucidate them. The whole meaning of Scripture is not upon the surface, and in the present connection we are expressly pointed to a symbolic signification in 1 Peter 3:20, 21; and the recurrence of the Ark as a sacred emblem in the great race-religions clearly indicates it as representing some universal principle.

The Zoroastrian legend of the flood throws some light upon the subject, for Yima, the Persian Noah, is bidden by Ahura Mazda, the Deity, to bring "the *seeds* of sheep, oxen, men and women, dogs and birds, and of every kind of tree and fruit, two of every kind, into the ark and to seal it up with a golden ring and make in it a door and a window." The significance of the Ark is that of a vehicle for the transmission of the life-principle of beings from an old to a new order of life, and all that is not included in the Ark perishes.

This is the generalized statement of relations which the Ark sets forth, and, like all other generalizations, it admits of a great many particular applications, ranging from those which are purely physiological to those which are in the highest degree spiritual, and the study of comparative religions will show us that the idea has been employed in all its most varied applications; yet, however varied, they all have this common feature: they signify something which conveys individual life safely through a period of transition from one order of manifestation to another.

The Ark, as the sacred vessel, plays a conspicuous part throughout Scripture, but in the present connection we shall best realize its meaning by considering it as the opposite principle to that from which it affords deliverance. If "Water" signifies the psychic principle, then the Ark signifies that which the psychic principle supports, and which has an opposite but correspondent nature—that is to say, the Body. The Ark is not independent of the Water but is constructed for the purpose of floating upon it, and similarly, the body is expressly adapted to man's psychic nature so as to make with it and the spiritual principle of Life a Whole individuality.

Now it is precisely in the recognition of this Wholeness that refuge from all psychic entanglements is to be found. We must always remember that the body equally with the soul is the instrument of the manifestation of the Spirit. It is the union of the three into a single Whole that constitutes the full reality of Life, and it is this sacredness of the body that is typified by the sacredness of the Ark. The Ark of Noah was a solid construction, built on a pattern all the details of which were laid down to scale by the Divine Architect and thus exemplifies the accurate proportions of the human body; and in passing it may interest the reader to note that the proportions of the human body numerically represent the principal measurements of the solar system and also form the basis of the proportions observed in such ecclesiastical architecture as is designed according to canonical rules, of which Westminster Abbey and Milan Cathedral are good examples.

I cannot, however, stop to digress into this very

interesting subject, and for our present purpose it will be sufficient to say that the Ark with its living freight is typical of the fact that the full *realization* of Life is only attained in the Threefold Unity of body, soul, and spirit, and not by their dissociation. It is the assertion of the solid, living Reality of the work of the Spirit as distinguished from those imperfect manifestations which are the subterranean roots of the true manifestation, but are not the real solid thing itself. It is the protest of healthy reality, which includes the psychic element *in its proper order* as the intermediary between the purely spiritual and the purely material, as against the rejection of the corporeal element and total absorption in the psychic—a condition which prevents the spirit from attaining to self-expression as a synthesis, which alone is the completion of its evolutionary work.

For this reason undue absorption in the psychic sphere is contrary to the Spirit; and however we may apply to it the word "spiritual" in the sense of not being corporeal, if the psychic element is not taken in its proper connection with the two others, it is as far from being "spiritual" in the true sense of the word as the material element itself. The true reality is in the harmonious interaction of the Three-in-ONE. God's world is a world of Truth in which evanescent shapes do not take the place of Reality, and for these reasons the Bible everywhere insists on nothing short of the fulness of perfect realization, and the Ark is one of the figures under which it does so.

This realization of the Triple Unity of Man is the first step towards our final enfranchisement; but in the very act of escaping from the danger of the Deluge we are exposed to a danger of the opposite kind, that of regarding the corporeal side of life as everything, and this is typified by the building of the Tower of Babel. This tower, note carefully, was built of brick—that is, of a substance which is nothing but clay, the same "red earth" out of which Adam is formed; and it is therefore the very opposite to the Heavenly Jerusalem, which is built of gold and precious stones.

Now a building naturally signifies a habitation, and the building of the Tower of Babel to escape the waters of a flood is that reaction against the psychic element which denies spiritual things altogether and makes of the body and its physical environment the one and only dwelling-place of man. It is the same error as before of trying to erect the edifice of Wholeness on the foundation merely of a part, only now the part selected is the corporeal instead of the psychic. Arithmetically it is the attempt to make out that one-third is the same as ONE. The natural consequences soon follow in the confusion of tongues.

Language is the expression of Thought, and if

our ideas of reality include nothing more than the infinitude of secondary causes which appear in the material world, there is no central Unit around which they can be grouped, and consequently, instead of any certain knowledge, we have only a multitude of conflicting opinions based upon the ever-changing aspects of the world of appearances. *Quot homines tot sententiae*;* and so the builders are dispersed in confusion, for theirs is not "the city that hath foundations whose builder and maker is God."†

From this point in the Bible story, a stretch of many ages brings us to the times of the Patriarchs Abraham, Isaac, and Jacob. We are here in the transition stage from allegory to history, and St. Paul points out this intermingling of the two elements when he tells us that Hagar and Sarah represent the two covenants and the earthly and heavenly Jerusalems. And here I would impress upon the student the dual character of scriptural personages and events. Because a personage or event is typical it does not follow that it is not also historical; on the contrary, certain personages, systems, and events, become typical—that is, specially emphasize certain principles, for the very reason

*"There are as many opinions as there are persons"—*Ed.*
†Hebrews 11:10—*Ed.*

that they give them concrete expression. As Johnson* says of the Swedish monarch:

He left the name at which the world grew pale,
To point a moral or adorn a tale.

In other words, historical realities become the very summing-up and visible form of abstract principles, and therefore we are justified by the Bible itself in finding in its personages types of principles as well as historical characters.

I will not, however, here open the question whether the three Patriarchs were actual personages, or, as some critics tell us, were merely the legendary ancestors of certain groups of wandering tribes, the Beni-Ibrahim, the Beni-Ishák, and the Beni-Yakub, which subsequently coalesced into the Hebrew nation. However interesting, the discussion of the historical facts would be remote from my present object, which is to throw some light upon the *inner* meaning of the Bible, and for this purpose we may be content to take the simple narrative of the text, for, whether actual or legendary, the only way in which Abraham, Isaac, and Jacob can affect us at the present day is as characters in

*Samuel Johnson (1709-1784), English lexicographer and author—*Ed.*

a history the significance of which will become clear if we read between the lines.

But from this latter point of view the biblical statement of the national origin of Israel carries enfolded within it the hidden statement of those great principles which it is the purpose of the Bible to reveal. And here let me draw attention to the method adopted in Scripture. There are certain great universal principles which permeate all planes of being from the highest to the lowest. They are not many in number, and the relations between them are not difficult of comprehension when clearly stated, but we find difficulty in recognizing the identity of the same principles when we meet with them, so to say, at different levels, as for example on the physical and the psychic planes respectively, and consequently we are apt to imagine them much more numerous and complicated than they really are.

Now, the purpose of the Bible is to convey instruction in the nature and use of these principles to those in whose hands this knowledge would be safe and useful, while concealing it from others; and in a manner appropriate to this object, it continually repeats the same few all-embracing principles over and over again. This repetition is firstly unavoidable because the principles themselves are few in number; next it is necessary as a process of hammering-in and fixing it in our minds; and lastly it is not a bare repetition, but there is a progressive expansion of the statement so as to conduct us step by step to a further comprehension of its meaning. Now this is done in a variety of ways, and one of frequent occurrence is through the use of Names.

Sacred Nomenclature is as large a study as Sacred Numeration, and indeed the two so shade off into one another that they may be regarded as forming a single study, and I will therefore no more attempt in the present book to elucidate the one system than the other, for they require a volume to themselves; but this need not prevent us considering occasional instances of both, and the names of the Patriarchs are too important to be passed over without notice. The frequency with which God is called in Scripture the God of Abraham, of Isaac, and of Jacob shows that something more must be referred to than the mere fact that the ancestors of the Jews worshipped Him, and the consideration of some of the prominent points in the history of these allegorical personages will throw a light on the subject which will be very helpful in our further investigation.

If we realize the truth of St. Paul's statement that the real object of the Bible is to convey the history of the spiritual Israel under the figure of Israel after the flesh, we shall see that the descent of

Israel from the three Patriarchs must be a spiritual descent, and we may therefore expect to find in the Patriarchs themselves an adumbration of the principles which give rise to the spiritual Israel. Now we should particularly notice that the name "Israel" was bestowed on Jacob, the third Patriarch, on the occasion when he wrestled with the angel at the ford Jabbok, and he obtained this name as the result of his successful wrestling. We are told that Jacob recognized that it was the Divine Being, the Nameless ONE, with whom he wrestled, and this at once gives us the key to the allegory; for we know from the Master's instruction to the woman of Samaria that God is Universal Spirit, and though the Universal is that which gives rise to all manifestations of the particular, yet it is logically and mathematically impossible for the Universal *as such* to assume individual personality.

Under the figure, therefore, of wrestling with "a man," we perceive that what Jacob wrestled with was the great problem of his own relation to the Universal Spirit under its twofold aspect of Universal Energy and Universal Intelligence, allegorically represented as a powerful man; and he held on and wrestled till he gained the blessing and the New Name in which the nature of that blessing was summed up. The conditions are significant. He was alone. Father of a large family as he was, none of his dear ones could help him in the struggle.

We must each solve the problem of our relation to the Infinite Mind for ourselves; and not our nearest and dearest can wrestle for us. And the struggle takes place in the darkness. It is when we begin to find that the light we thought we possessed is not the true light, when we find that its illuminating power is gone, that we rise nerved with an energy we never knew before and commence in earnest the struggle for the Light, determined never to let go until we win the victory. And so we wrestle till the day begins to break, but even then we must not quit our hold; we must not be content until we have received the New Name which marks our possession of that principle of Light and Life which will forever expand into brighter day and fuller livingness. "To him that overcometh will I give . . . a New Name" (Rev. 2:17).

But Jacob carries with him the mark of the struggle throughout his earthly career. The angel touched the hollow of his thigh, and thenceforward he was lame. The meaning is simple enough to those who have had some experience of the wrestling. They can never again walk in earthly things with the same step as before. They have seen the Truth, and they can never again unsee it; their whole *standpoint* has been altered and is no longer understood by those around them; to those who have not wrestled with the angel, they appear to walk lamely.

What, then, was the New Name that was thus gained by the resolute wrestler? His original name of Jacob was changed to Israel. The definition given of Israel in the seventy-third Psalm is "such as are of a clean heart," and Jesus expressed the same idea when he said of Nathanael, "Behold an Israelite indeed in whom is no guile"; for the emphasis laid upon the word "Israelite" at once suggests some inner meaning, since Nathanael's nationality was no more remarkable under the circumstances than that of an Englishman in Piccadilly.

The great fact about the spiritual Israel is therefore cleanness of heart and absence of guile—in other words, perfect sincerity, which again implies singleness of purpose in the right direction. It is precisely that quality which our Buddhist friends call "one-pointedness," and on which, under various similitudes, the Master laid so much stress. This, then, is the distinctive characteristic which attaches to the name of Israel, for it is this *concentration* of effort that is the prime factor in gaining the victory which leads to the acquisition of the Name. This is fundamental, and without it nothing can be accomplished; it indicates the sort of mental character which we must aim at, but it is not the meaning of the Name itself.

The name of Israel is composed of three syllables, each of which carries a great meaning. The first syllable, "Is," is primarily the sound of the indrawing of the breath, and hence acquires the significance of the Life-Principle in general, and more particularly of individual Life. This recognition of the individualization of the Life-Principle formed the basis of the Assyrian worship. The syllable "Is" was also rendered "As," "Ish," and "Ash" and gave rise to the worship of the Life-Principle under the plural name "Ashur," which thus represented the male and female elements, the former being worshipped as Ashr, or Asr, and the latter as Ashré, Ashira, Astarte, Iastara or Ishtar, a lunar goddess of Babylon, and the same idea of femininity is found in the Egyptian "Isis."

Hence the general conception conveyed by the syllable "Is" is that of a feminine spiritual principle manifesting itself in individuality—that is to say, the "Soul" or formative element—and it is thus indicative of all that we mean when we speak of the psychic side of nature. How completely the Assyrians identified themselves with the cultus of this principle is shown by the name of their country, which is derived from "Ashur."

The second syllable, "Ra," is the name of the great Egyptian sun-god and is thus the complementary of everything that is signified by "Is." It is primarily indicative of physical life rather than psychic life, and in general represents the Universal Life-giving power as distinguished from its manifestation in particular individuality. Ra symbolizes the Sun, while Is is symbolized by the Moon, and represents the masculine element as emphatically as Is represents the feminine.

The third syllable, "El," has the significance of Universal Being. It is "THE"—i.e., the nameless Principle, which includes in itself both the masculine and feminine elements, both the physical and the psychic, and is greater than them and gives rise to them. It is another form of the word Al, Alé, or Ala, which means "High," and is indicative of the Supreme Principle *before it passes into any differentiated mode*. It is *pure* Spirit in the *universal*.

Now, if Man is to attain liberty, it can only be by the realization of these Three Modes of Being—the physical, the psychic, and the spiritual; or, as the Bible expresses it, Body, Soul, and Spirit. He must know what these three are in himself and must also recognize the Source from which they spring, and he must at least have some moderately definite idea of their genesis into individuality.

Therefore the man "instructed unto the kingdom of heaven" combines a threefold recognition of himself and of God which is accurately represented by the combination of the three syllables Is, Ra, and El. Unless these three are joined into a single unity, a single word, the recognition is incomplete and the full knowledge of truth has not been attained. "Ra" by itself implies only the knowledge of the physical world, and results in Materialism. "Is" by itself realizes only the psychic world, and results in Sorcery. "El" by itself corresponds only with a vague apprehension of some overruling power, capricious and devoid of the element of Law, and thus results in Idolatry.

It is only in the combination of all three elements that the true Reality is to be found, whether we study it in its physical, psychic, or spiritual aspect. We may for particular purposes give special prominence to one aspect over the two others, but this is for a time only, and even while we do so, we realize that the particular mode of Life-Power with which we are dealing derives its efficiency only from the fact of its being permeated by the other two.

We cannot too firmly impress upon our minds that, though there are *three modes*, there is only ONE LIFE; and in all our studies, and in their practical application, we must never forget the great truth that the Living Power which we use is a Synthesis, and that whenever we make an analysis we theoretically destroy the synthesis. The only purpose of making an analysis is to learn how to build up the synthesis; and it is for this reason that the Bible equally condemns the opposite extremes of materialism and sorcery. It tells us that "dogs and sorcerers" are excluded from the heavenly city, and when we understand what is meant by these terms, it becomes self-evident that it cannot be otherwise.

It is for this reason, also, that we find the Israelites so often warned both against the Babylonian and the Egyptian idolatries; not because there was no great underlying truth in the worship of those nations, but because it was a worship that excluded the idea of WHOLENESS. "Wilt thou be made whole?" is the Divine invitation to us all; and the Egyptian and Assyrian worships were eminently calculated to lead their votaries away from this Wholeness in opposite directions.

But that both the Assyrian and the Egyptian worship had a solid basis of truth is a fact to which the Bible itself bears this remarkable testimony: "In that day shall Israel be the third with Egypt and with Assyria, even a blessing in the midst of the land; whom the Lord of Hosts shall bless, saying, Blessed be Egypt my people, and Assyria the work of my hands, and Israel mine inheritance" (Isaiah

19:24,25). The Israelite worship was as essentially that of the principle represented by "El" as those of Egypt and Assyria were of the two others, and it needed the balancing of those two extremes by the recognition of their relation to the central, or spiritual, principle to constitute the realization of the true Divine Sonship of Man in which no element of this threefold being—body, soul, or spirit—is alien from unity with "the Father."

This, then, was the significance of the New Name given to Jacob. He had wrestled with the Divine until the light had begun to dawn upon him, and he thus acquired the right to a name which should correctly describe what he had now become. Formerly he had been Jacob—i.e, Yakub, a name derived from the root "Yak" or "One." This signifies the third stage of apprehension of the Divine problem which immediately precedes the final discovery of the great secret of the Trinity-in-Unity of Being. We realize the ONE-ness of the Universal Divine Principle, though we have not yet realized its Threefold nature both in ourselves and in the Universal.

But there are two other stages before this, the first of which is represented by Abraham and the second by Isaac. It should be noted that the two syllables "Ra" and "Is" reappear in these names, the former indicative, as we have seen, of the masculine element of Spirit, and the latter of the feminine, while Jacob, or simple unity, is indicative of the neuter.

If we look through the history of Abraham we find the masculine element especially predominant in it. He is the *father* of the nations that are to spring from him, he receives the covenant of circumcision, he is a warrior and goes forth to victorious battle, and the change of his name from Abram to Abraham is the substitution of a masculine for a neuter element.

In Isaac's history the feminine element is equally predominant. His name is connected with the laughter of his mother (Genesis 18), and his marriage with Rebekah is the pivot round which all the events of his life center; and again, his acquiescence in his own sacrifice marks the predominance of the passive element in his character. To him there comes no change of name; he is neither leader, warrior, nor spiritual wrestler, but the calm, contemplative man who "went out to meditate in the field at eventide"; he is typical of the purely receptive attitude of mind, and therefore the syllable "Is" is as indicative of his nature as the masculine syllable "Ra" is of his father's, or the neutral and purely mathematical conception indicated by the syllable "Yak" is of his son's.

This affords a good instance of the way in which

the deepest truths are often concealed in Bible names, and it should lead us to see that the value of the record does not turn on its literal accuracy at every point, but on its correct representation of the great principles to the knowledge of which it seeks to lead us.

It is of little moment to us at the present date how much of the book of Genesis is legendary and how much historical, and we can afford to view calmly such little inaccuracies on the face of the document as when we are told, in Exodus 6:3, that God was not known to Abraham by the name Jehovah, and in Genesis 22:14, that Abraham called the place where he was delivered from sacrificing Isaac "Jehovah-jireh." There are two typical schools of Biblical interpretation, one of which is historically represented by St. Augustine and the other by St. Jerome. Augustine, who was not an Orientalist and had not studied the original Hebrew, took his stand upon the textual accuracy of the Bible and urged that if once any inaccuracy were admitted to exist in it, we could never be certain of anything in the whole book. Jerome, who had made an accurate study of the original Hebrew, admitted the existence of inaccuracies in the text from the operation of the same natural causes which affect other ancient literature, such as errors of copyists, variations of oral tradition, and even possible adaptation to the requirements of something which the transcriber believed to be an essential doctrine.

These two representative men were not separated by an interval of centuries but were contemporaries and actually in communication with each other, and we may therefore see from how early a date Christendom has been divided into blind reverence for the letter and intelligent inquiry into the history of its documents. St. Jerome was the father of the Higher Criticism, and with such a respectable authority to back us, we need not be afraid to attribute any such casual errors as the one now in question to those natural causes which render all ancient documents liable to variation, and the point to which I would draw attention is that merely superficial contradictions which can be reasonably accounted for on purely natural grounds in no way affect the general inspiration of the Bible.

And by "inspiration" I mean an inner illumination on the part of the writers leading them to the immediate perception of Truth, which illumination is itself a fact in the regular order of Nature, the reason of which I hope to make clear in a subsequent volume. The books of the Pentateuch, as we possess them, were written by Ezra and his scribes after the return from the Babylonian captivity—those writers whom the Jews call "the men of the Great Synagogue," and whose writings were separated from the time of Moses by exactly the same interval that separates Tennyson's *Idylls of the King* from the date of the actual King Arthur.

This alone leaves a sufficiently wide margin for errors to creep into such earlier documents as these writers may have availed themselves of; and we must next reflect that another interval of several centuries separated them from the copies conveyed to Egypt in the second century before Christ for Ptolemy Soter's* Greek translation, commonly known as the Septuagint. The "Temple Standard" Pentateuch, preserved at Jerusalem at the time of Jesus, can hardly have been the original document written by Ezra, but even supposing it to have been so, what became of it at the destruction of Jerusalem? Tradition says it was sent by Josephus to the Emperor of Rome; and written, as it is said to have been, on bulls' hides, we may well imagine that it perished by damp or other agencies, neglected as a barbarous relic in a city whose energies were concentrated on maintaining its position as arbitress of the world by conquest and diplomacy; at any rate,

*(366?–283? B.C.), King of Egypt and founder of the famous library of Alexandria—*Ed.*

the document was never heard of again, and the oldest Jewish versions of the Pentateuch now extant are not older than the tenth century.

Under these circumstances we need not be surprised if variations have found their way into the text nor need we trouble ourselves much about them if we reflect that the real place where Truth exists is in Nature, and not in books, and that the book is merely a record of what others have learnt without book; and, moreover, owing to the deep reverence with which both Jewish and Christian Scriptures have been preserved, we may say that any errors or contradictions discovered in the text no more affect the body of the Truth contained in the Bible as a whole than the dust on the outside of an orange affects the value of the fruit. It is this *inner* Truth that we are seeking, and if we at all realize the Master's statement that the Kingdom is *within*, superficial discrepancies will not present any difficulties to us.

We see, then, in the typical history of the three Patriarchs the announcement of the three great principles into which all forms of manifestation may be analysed: the Masculine, Positive, or generating principle; the Feminine, Receptive, or formative principle; and the Neuter or Mathematical principle, which, by determining the proportional relations between the other two, gives rise to the principle of variety and multiplicity.

Their successive statement in the symbolical history indicates the need for the preparatory study of each in detail if we would arrive at the True Light; and it is precisely the discovery that this separate study is by itself *insufficient* that brings us to the point where we have to wrestle in the darkness with the Divine Angel until the day dawns. We must unite the three principles into a single Unity, and thus learn to form the name "Israel"; and in so doing we discover that it has now become *our own* name, for we find that the kingdom of heaven—the realm of eternal principles—is *within* us, and that therefore whatever we discover there, is that which we ourselves are.

Our wrestling ceases: the Divine Wrestler has put his name upon us, and the day is beginning to dawn; but as yet it is only the earliest hour of daybreak; it is the true sunlight, but it is still low on the horizon, and we must not make the mistake of supposing that this early morning hour is the same as the mid-day glory—in other words, we must not suppose that because we have once and forever finished wrestling with an unknown antagonist in darkness, therefore we have nothing more to do.

Life is a perpetual *doing*, though, thank God,

not a perpetual wrestling. Our doing is the measure of our living, although the plane on which our doing is carried on may not be immediately patent to all observers; and it is exactly in proportion as we expand our doing that we expand our livingness. No one can grow for us, and it all depends upon ourselves how rapidly and how strongly we shall grow.

CHAPTER 4

The Mission of Moses

Having now gathered up in the briefest possible fashion the general gist of the history of the Patriarchs, we must pass on to the Mission of Moses. And here let me again impress upon the reader that the Bible repeats its few grand principles over and over again, only with greater detail as it proceeds, so that we shall find precisely the same principles involved in the history of the march of Israel into Canaan as in that of the three Patriarchs. It is the same statement as is contained in the story of Eden and in the tradition of the Flood, and we shall find it repeated throughout the Bible under other varieties of form which admit of more and more specific application of these principles to individual cases. I mention this to explain why we may sometimes appear to go over old ground: there is only ONE Truth, and more detailed acquaintance with it will not change its fundamentals.

We have seen that the Bible teaching regarding Man starts with two great facts: first, that he is the image of God, reproducing in individuality the same Universal Mind which is the Origin of all things, and thus reproducing also its creative process of Thought; and, secondly, that he is ignorant of this truth, and so brings upon himself all sorts of trouble and limitation; and it is the purpose of the Bible to lead us step by step out of this ignorance into this knowledge—step by step, for it is a process of growth, first in the individual, then in the race, and this growth depends on certain clear and ascertainable Laws inherent in the constitution of Man. Now the peculiarity of inherent Law is that it always acts uniformly, making no exception in favor of anyone, and it does this as well positively as negatively.

Our ignorance of any Law of Nature will never exempt us from its operation, and this is as true of ignorant obedience as of ignorant disobedience; the natural reward of ignorant obedience is no less certain than the natural punishment of ignorant disobedience; and it is on this principle that the great leaders of the race have always worked. They themselves knew the Law; but to impart the understanding of the Law to people in general was not the work of a day, nor of a generation, nor of many generations—in fact it is a work which is still only in its infancy—and therefore if people were to be saved from the consequences of disobedience to the Law, it could only be by some method of training which would lead them into ignorant obedience to it.

But this was not to be done by making any false statement of the Law, for Truth can never come out of falsehood; it must be done by presenting the Truth under such figures as would indicate the real relations of things, though not explaining how these relations arise, because to undeveloped minds such an explanation would be worse than useless. Hence came the whole system of the Mosaic Law.

On one occasion, when the Master was asked which was the greatest commandment of the Law, He replied by quoting the fourth verse of the sixth chapter of Deuteronomy, "Hear, O Israel: the Lord our God is one Lord," or, as the Revised Version has it in Mark 12:29, "the Lord is ONE." This, He says, is the first of all the commandments; and we may therefore expect to find in this statement of the Divine Unity the foundation on which everything else rests. Nor need we look far to find the reason of it, for we have already seen in the opening words of Genesis that *in principio*—that is, as the originating principle in all things—there *can* be nothing else but God or Spirit. That is a conclusion which becomes unavoidable if we simply follow up the chain of cause and effect until we reach a Universal First Cause. We may call it by what name we choose: that will make no difference so long as we realize what *must* be its inherent nature and what *must* be our necessary relation to it.

Whatever name we give it, it is always the ONE Self-existent and Self-transforming Power of which everything is some mode of manifestation, simply because there is no other source from which anything could come. This ultimate deduction of reason is the recognition of the Unity of God and could not be more clearly stated than in the words which Isaiah puts into the mouth of the Divine Being, repeating the phrase in two consecutive sentences as though to lay additional stress upon it: "There is none beside Me. . . . I am God, and there is none else" (Isaiah 45:21,22). That is to say, "God" —or, as we have learnt from the instructions to the woman of Samaria, Universal Spirit—is all that is.

This is the great Truth on which the mission of Moses was founded, and therefore that mission starts with the announcement of the Divine Name at the Burning Bush. "Moses said unto God, Behold, when I come unto the children of Israel, and shall say unto them, The God of your fathers hath sent me unto you; and they shall say to me, What is His name? what shall I say unto them? And God said unto Moses, I AM THAT I AM; and He said,

Thus shalt thou say unto the children of Israel, I AM hath sent me unto you."

So the name after which Moses inquired turned out to be no name, but the first person singular of the present tense of the verb TO BE, in its indicative mood. It is the announcement of BEING in the Absolute, in that first originating plane of Pure Spirit where, because the Material does not yet exist, there can be no extension in space, and consequently no sequence in time, and where therefore the only possible mode of being is the consciousness of Self-existence without limitation either of space or time, the realization of the "universal Here and the everlasting Now," the concentration of the All into the Point and the expansion of the Point into the All.*

But though this may have been a new announcement to the masses of the Hebrew people, it could have been no new announcement to Moses, for we are told in the Acts that Moses was learned in all the wisdom of the Egyptians, a circumstance which is fully accounted for by his education at the court of Pharaoh, where he would be as a matter of course initiated into the deepest mysteries of the Egyptian religion. He must therefore have been

*For further elucidation the reader is referred to my *Edinburgh Lectures on Mental Science*.

familiar from boyhood with the words "I AM that I AM," which as the inscription "Nuk pu Nuk" appeared upon the walls of every temple; and having received the highest instruction in the land, brought up as the son of Pharaoh's daughter, he must have been well aware of their significance. But this instruction had hitherto been confined to those who had been initiated into the great mysteries of Osiris.

In whatever way we may interpret the story of Moses' meeting with the Divine Being at the burning bush, one thing is evident: it indicates the point in his career when it became plain to him that the only possible way for the Liberation of mankind was through the universal recognition of that Truth which till now had been the exclusive secret of the sanctuaries. What, then, was the great central Truth which was thus announced in this proclamation of the Divine Name? It has two sides to it. First, that Pure Spirit is the ultimate essence of all that is, and as a consequence the All-presence, the All-knowledge, the All-livingness, and the All-lovingness of "God." Then as the corollary of the proposition that "Spirit is all that is," there must be the converse proposition that "'all that is is Spirit"; and since Man is included in the "all," we are again brought back to the original description of him as the image and likeness of God.

But in those days people had to be educated up to these two great truths, and they have not advanced very far in this education yet; so from the time when Moses' eyes were opened to see in these truths not a secret to be guarded for his private benefit, but the power which was to expand to the renovation of the world, he realized that it was his mission to set men free by educating them gradually into the true knowledge of the Divine Name. Then he conceived a great scheme.

Modern research has shown us that the knowledge of this great fundamental truth was not confined to Egypt, but formed the ultimate centre of all the religions of antiquity; it was that secret in which the supreme initiation of all the highest mysteries culminated. It could not be otherwise, for it was the only ultimate conclusion to which generations of clear-headed thinkers could come. But these were sages, priests, philosophers, men of education and leisure; and this final deduction was beyond the reach of the toiling multitudes, whose whole energies had to be devoted to the earning of their daily bread.

Still, it was impossible for these thinkers who *had* arrived at the great knowledge to pass over the multitudes without allowing them at least a few crumbs from their table. The true recognition of the "Self" must always carry with it the purpose of helping others to acquire it also; but it does not necessarily imply the immediate perception of the best means of doing so, and hence throughout antiquity we find an inner religion, the Supreme Mysteries, for the initiated few; and an outer religion, for the most part idolatrous, for the people. The people were not to be left without any religion, but they were given a religion which was deemed suited to their gross apprehension of things; and in the hands of lower orders of priests—themselves little, if at all, better instructed than the worshippers—these conceptions often became very gross indeed. Nevertheless, in their first intention the "idols" were not without meaning.

The cultured Greeks laughed at the Egyptian temples as places where, in the midst of a magnificent edifice, when the sacred curtain of the innermost sanctuary was withdrawn, there was revealed an onion or a cat. Yet here was surely enough to prompt an intelligent person to enquiry. Why did the innermost sanctuary contain no Apollo Belvedere or other marvel unique and worthy to be enshrined, but only one of those wretched animals which disturbed the rest of the Greek traveller, newly arrived in Egypt, by nocturnal caterwaulings which must have been a marked feature in cities where pussy held undisputed sway? Or why was the odoriferous onion that lay by tons for sale in the markets here set up upon a pedestal as an object of reverence? Surely there must be some deep significance in elevating such common objects to the central place of mystery. Yes: because in these commonest of common things there appeared the Great Central Mystery of LIFE more than in the sculptured marble of Phidias or Praxiteles.

Thus the Egyptian religion signified, to all who had the "nous"* to penetrate it, the All-presence of the Eternal Living Spirit as the ONE true object of worship, to be found, not only in temples, but in streets and fields, in all places alike. It signified this to those who had the intelligence to lift the veil, and this meant, perhaps, one in ten thousand of the population; and as soon as he had penetrated the real meaning, his lips were sealed, for he was admitted to the Mysteries. For the rest, the priests had such trivial superficial explanations as those which ages later they sought to palm off upon Herodotus; it was no part of their business to lift the veil of Isis.

And so Moses saw the generations toiling on and on in an ignorance which could not but have disastrous consequences sooner or later. Under the paternal rule of a truly illuminated priesthood, such a relation between the inner and the outer

*(In British usage) "alertness"—*Ed.*

religion might be employed to maintain a condition of peaceful well-being for the masses during their intellectual infancy; but he saw that this state of things could not go on indefinitely.

With a general advance in intelligence must come a general disposition to question the outward forms of religion, while yet this general advance fell very far short of that fuller development which in solitary instances led the individual to grasp the meaning of the inner Truth. Then, when to any nation comes the ridicule of all it has hitherto held sacred, because it has never learnt the Eternal Truth itself but has placed its faith in forms and ceremonies and traditions, which, useful in their day and generation, should have been unfolded to meet growing intelligence—when this condition of the national mind supervenes, woe to that nation, for it is left without God and without hope, and by the inevitable Law of Nature on the plane of MIND, it cannot but bring upon itself dire calamity.

From the standpoint of the governed, this benign, paternal government could not go on forever, and equally so from that of the rulers. What guarantee was there of a perpetual succession of priests illuminated not only in head but also in heart? Egypt was old when Moses was a youth, and the signs of decadence were not wanting; for the cruel oppression of the Israelites, whom four centuries of naturalization should have placed on equality with their fellow-subjects, was the very reverse of all that was truest in the inner teaching of the Egyptian temples. It was the index of practical atheism. The Science of the temples continued, but it had reached the bifurcation of the Way, and it had taken the Left-hand Path.

And if this was the case in Egypt, which led the van of civilization, what was to be expected from the rest of the world? What was the outlook into the future with an intellectual development expanding only on the material side, without any knowledge of those spiritual truths in which lies the real livingness of Life? Surely nothing but the ultimate destruction of mankind in internecine strife, led up to by long ages of that awful spiritual condition in which the outward polish of materialized intellectuality only serves to place additional resources at the disposal of the unmitigated savage within.

The system then in vogue had once been a valuable system, perhaps the only one possible, but Egypt was no longer young, and the day of that system had palpably gone by. What was to be done? That great central Truth which the old system had handed down from hoary antiquity must be made the common appanage of mankind. "Nuk-pu-Nuk"* must no longer be the mysterious legend of the temples, but it must become the household word of every family thoughout the world.

This is the work of generation upon generation, very far from being accomplished yet; and the only way to inaugurate it was by a new departure in which the great announcement that had hitherto been reserved as the last and final teaching must become the first and initial teaching. The supreme secret of the Mysteries must be made the starting-point of the child's education; and therefore the mission to Israel must open with the declaration of the I AM as the All-embracing ONE.

A sentence consists of a subject, copula,† and predicate, but in the announcement of the Divine Name made to Moses, there is no predicate. The reason is that to predicate anything of a subject implies some special aspect of it, and thus by implication *limits* it, however extensive the predicate may be; and it is impossible to apply this mode of statement to the Universal Living Spirit. There can be nothing *outside* it. Itself is the Substance and the

*See p. 82—*Ed.*

†A verb, such as *be, seem,* that links a subject with its predicate (the part of the sentence that expresses what is said of the subject)—*Ed. (Merriam-Webster Dictionary)*

Life of all that is or ever can be. That is an ultimate conception from which it is impossible to get away.

Therefore, the only predicate corresponding to the Universal Subject must be the enumeration of the innumerable—the statement of all that is contained in infinite possibility—and, consequently, the place of the predicate must be left apparently unfilled, because it is that fulness which includes *all*. The only possible statement of the Divine is that of Present Subjective Being, the Universal "I" and the ever-present "AM." Therefore I AM is the Name of God; and the First of all the Commandments is the announcement of the Divine Being as the Infinite ONE.

I have discussed the subject of the Unity of Spirit in my *Edinburgh Lectures on Mental Science*, but I may repeat here the truth that, mathematically, the Infinite *must* be Unity. We cannot think of two Infinites, for as soon as duality appears, each member of it is limited by the other, else there would be no duality. Therefore we cannot multiply the Infinite. Similarly, we cannot divide it, for division again implies multiplicity or Numbers, and though these may be conceived of as existing relatively to each other *within* the Infinite, the very relation between them establishes limits where one begins and the other ends, and thus we are no longer dealing with the Infinite.

Of course all this is self-evident to the mathematician, who at once sees the absurdity of attempting to multiply or divide infinity; but the nonmathematical reader should endeavor to realize the full meaning of the word "Infinite" as that which, being without limits, necessarily occupies all space and therefore includes all that is. The announcement that God is ONE is, therefore, the mathematical statement of the Universal Presence of Spirit, and the phrase "I AM" is the grammatical statement of the same thing.

And because the Universal Spirit is the Universal Life Itself, "over all, through all, and in all," there is yet a third statement of it, which is its Living statement: the reproduction of it in the man himself; and these three statements are one and cannot be separated. Each implies the two others, like the three sides of an equilateral triangle, and therefore the First of all the Commandments is that we shall recognize THE ONE. As numerically all other numbers are developed from unity, so all the possibilities of ever-expanding Life are developed from the All-including UNIT of Being, and therefore in this Commandment we find the root of our future growth to all eternity. This is why both Moses and Jesus assign to it the supreme place.

And here let me point out the intimate relation between the teaching of Jesus and the teaching of

Moses. They are the two great figures of the Bible. As the Old Testament centres round the one, so the New Testament centres round the other. Each appeals to the other. Moses says, "Of thy brethren, shall the Lord thy God raise up a prophet *like unto me*"—the prophet that was to come should duplicate Moses; and when that prophet came, he said, "If they hear not Moses and the prophets, neither will they be persuaded though one rose from the dead." Each is the complement of the other. We shall never understand Jesus until we understand Moses, and we shall never understand Moses until we understand Jesus.

Yet this is not a paradox, for to grasp the meaning of either we must find the key to their utterances in our own hearts, and on our own lips in the words "I AM"; that is, we must go back to that Divine Universal Law of Being which is written within us, and of which both Moses and Jesus were the inspired exponents.

The mission of Moses, then, was to build up a nationality which should be independent both of time and country, and which should derive its solidarity from its recognition of the principle of THE ONE. Its national being must be based upon its expanding realization of the great central Truth, and to the guarding and developing of that Truth this nation must be consecrated; and in the enslaved but not subdued children of the desert—the children of Israel—Moses found ready to hand the material which he needed. For these erstwhile wanderers had brought with them a simple monotheistic creed, a belief in the God of Abraham, Isaac, and Jacob, which, vaguely though it might be, already touched the threshold of the sacred mystery; and four hundred years of residence in Egypt had not extinguished, however it may have obscured, the great tradition. Here, then, Moses found the nucleus for the nationality he designed to found, and so he led forth the people in that great symbolic march through the wilderness whose story is told in the Exodus.

To the details of that history we may turn more intelligently after we have gained a clearer idea of what the great work really was which Moses inaugurated on the night of the first Passover. Perhaps some of my readers may be surprised to learn that it is still going on and that they are called upon to take a personal part in continuing the work of Moses, which has now so expanded as to reach themselves.

But all this is contained in the commission which Moses first announced to those he was to deliver and grows naturally out of its unfoldment. The people he was to lead into liberty were "the people of God," and since "God" is the I AM, they were "THE PEOPLE OF THE I AM." This was the true Name of this nation, which was to be founded upon an Eternal Ideal instead of on the historical conditions of time and the geographical conditions of place; and this *essential* name of the New Nation has been as accurately translated into its equivalent of "Israel" as we shall later see the *essential* Name of God has been translated by the word "Jehovah." "The People of God" led forth by Moses were proclaimed by the very terms of his commission to be "The People of the I AM."

Now the history of this people is dignified by a succession of Prophets such as no other nation lays claim to; yet the great Prophet who first consolidated their scattered tribes into a compact community, in prophesying of the future of the people he had founded, passes over all these and, looking down the long centuries, points only to one other Prophet "like unto me." We constantly miss those little indications of Scripture on which the fuller understanding of it so greatly depends; and just as we miss the point when we are told that Man is created in the likeness of God, so we miss the point when we are told that this other Prophet, Jesus, is a Prophet of the same type as Moses.

The whole line of intervening prophets were not

of that type. They had their own special work, but it was not a work like that of Moses. Isaiah, Jeremiah, Ezekiel, and the rest sink out of sight, and the only Prophet whom Moses sees in the future is brought into his field of vision by His likeness to himself. Any child in a Sunday school, if asked what it knew about Moses, would answer that he brought the children of Israel out of Egypt. No one would question that this was the distinctive fact regarding him, and therefore if we are to find a Prophet of the same type as Moses, we should expect to find in Him the founder of a New Nationality of the same order as that founded by Moses—that is to say, a nationality subsisting independently of time and place and cohering by reason of its recognition of an Eternal Ideal.

To make Jesus a Prophet like unto Moses, he must in some way repeat the Exodus and reestablish "the people of the I AM." Now turning to the teaching of Jesus, we find that this is exactly what He did. There was nothing on which He laid greater stress than the I AM. "Except ye believe that I AM, ye shall perish in your sins" was the emphatic summary of His whole teaching. And here read carefully. Distinguish between what Jesus said and what the translators of our English Bible say that He said, for it makes all the difference. Our English version runs, "If ye believe not that I am *He*, ye shall die in your sins" (John 8:24), thus, by the introduction of a single word, assuming all sorts of theological doctrines having their origin in Persian and Neoplatonic speculations, the discussion of which would require a volume to itself. Not false doctrines, but great truths are presented in such infantine notions as to convey the most limiting conception of ideals whose vitality consists in their transcending all limitations.

Thus both as theologians and grammarians the translators of the Authorized Version felt the want of a predicate to complete the words I AM, and so they added the word "*he*"; but, faithful according to their light, they were careful to draw attention to the fact that there was no "he" in the original, and therefore that word is printed in italics to show that it was supplied by the translators; and the Revised Version carefully notes this fact in the margin.

In the parallel case of the announcement to Moses at the burning bush, the translators did not attempt to introduce any predicate; they felt what I have pointed out: that no predicate could be sufficiently extensive to define Infinite Being; but here, supposing that Jesus was speaking of Himself personally, they thought it necessary to introduce a word which should limit His statement accordingly. Now the only comment to be made on this passage of the English Bible is to note carefully that it is exactly what Jesus *never said*. In this connection He made no personal application of the verb "to be." What he said was, "Except ye believe that I AM, ye shall die in your sins" (R. V.). Now, if the criterion by which we are to recognize Him as the Prophet predicted by Moses is His reproduction of the doings of Moses, then we cannot be wrong in supposing that His use of the I AM was as complete a *generalization* as was employed by Moses.

On the same principle on which theologians or grammarians would particularize the words to the individuality of Jesus, they might particularize them to Moses also. But going back to that generalized statement of Man which is the very first intimation the Bible gives of him, we find that if I AM is the generalized statement of "God," it must also be the generalized statement of "Man," for man is the image and likeness of God. Whatever is true of one is true of the other, only conversely, and, as it were, by reflection; so that whatever is universal in God becomes individual in man.

If, then, Jesus was to duplicate the work of Moses, it could only be by taking as the foundation of His teaching the same statement of *essential* Being that Moses took as the foundation of his; and therefore we must look for a generic, and not for a specific, application of the I AM in his teaching also. And as soon as we do this, the veil is lifted and a power streams forth from all his instructions which shows us that it was no mere figure of speech when He said that the water which He should give would become, in each one who drank of it, a well of water springing up into everlasting life. He came not to proclaim Himself, but Man; not to tell us of His Own Divinity separating Him from the race and making Him the Great Exception, but to tell us of *our* Divinity and to show in Himself the Great Example of the I AM reaching its full personal expression in Man.

This Prophet is raised up "of our brethren," He is one of ourselves, and therefore He said, "The disciple when he is perfected shall be *as his Master*." It is the Universal I AM reproducing itself in the individuality of Man that Jesus would have us believe in. He is preaching nothing but the same old Truth with which the Bible begins, that Man is the image and likeness of God. He says, in effect, Make this recognition the centre of your life and you have tapped the source of everlasting life; but refuse to believe it and you will die in your sins. Why? As a Divine vengeance upon you for daring to question a theological formulary to which some narrow-minded ecclesiastic applies the words of the

Vincentian canon, "Quod semper, quod ubique, quod ab omnibus,"* when his formulary has never even been heard of outside such limits as both historically and geographically give the lie direct to his assertion of "always," "everywhere," and "by all men"? Certainly not. Truth has a surer foundation than forms of words; it is deep down in the foundations of Being; and it is the failure to realize this Truth of Being *in ourselves* that is the refusal to believe in the I AM which must necessarily cause us to perish in our sins. It is not a theological vengeance, but the Law of Nature. Let us enquire, then, what this Law is.

It is the great Law that, to live at all, we must primarily live in ourselves. No one can live for us. We can never get away from being the centre of our own world; or, in scientific language, our life is essentially subjective. There could be no objective life without a subjective entity to receive the perceptions which the objective faculties convey to it; and since the receiving entity is ourself, the only life possible to us is that of living in our own perceptions. Whatever we believe, does, for us, in very fact exist.

*The theologian Vincent of Lérins (d. before A.D. 450), in his *Commonitoria*, devised a formula for determining theological orthodoxy. Known as the Vincentian Canon, the formula emphasizes tradition, defining orthodoxy as "What has been believed always, everywhere, and by all men."—*Ed.*

Our beliefs may be erroneous from the standpoint of a happier belief, but this does not alter the fact that for ourselves our beliefs are our realities, and these realities must continue until some ground is found for a change in belief.

And in turn, the subjective entity reacts upon the objective life, for if there is one fact which the advance of modern psychological science is making more clear than another it is that the subjective entity is "the builder of the body." And this is precisely what, on the information we have already gleaned from the Bible, it ought to be; for we have seen that the statement that Man is the image of God can only be interpreted as a statement of his having in himself the same creative process of Thought to which alone it is possible to attribute the origin of anything. He is the image of God because he is the individualization of the Universal Mind at that stage of self-evolution in which the individual attains the capacity for reasoning from the seen to the unseen, and thus for penetrating behind the veil of outward appearances; so that, because of the reproduction of the Divine creative faculty in himself, the man's mental states or modes of thought are bound to externalize themselves in his body and his circumstances.

This, then, is the Law of Man's Being. I do not stop to discuss it in detail, as, writing for New

Thought readers, I assume at least an elementary knowledge of these things on their part; and accordingly, this being the Law, we see that the more closely our conception of ourselves approximates to a *broad generalization* of the factors which go to make human personality, rather than that narrow conception which limits our notion of ourselves to certain particular relations that have gathered around us, the more fully we shall externalize *this* idea of ourselves. And because the idea is a *generalization* independent of any particular circumstance, it must necessarily externalize as a corresponding independence of circumstances; in other words, it must result in a control over conditions, whether of body or environment, proportioned to the completeness of our generalization.

The more perfect the generalization, the more perfect the corresponding control over conditions; and therefore to attain the most complete control, which means the most perfect Liberty, we need to conceive of ourselves as embodying the idea of the most perfect generalization. But complete generalization is only another expression for infinitude, and therefore we have again reached the point where it becomes impossible to attach any predicate to the verb "to Be"; and so the only statement which contains the whole Law of Man's Being is identical with the only statement which contains the whole Law of God's Being, and consequently I AM is as much the correct formula for Man as for God.

But if we do not believe this and make it the centre of our life, we must perish in our sins. The Bible defines "sin" as "the transgression of the Law," and Jesus' warning is that by transgressing the Law of our own Being, we shall die. It would carry me beyond the general lines of this book to discuss the question of what is here meant by "Death"; but that it is not the everlasting damnation of the Western creeds is obvious from the single statement of the Bible, that the Master employed the interval between His death and resurrection in teaching those souls who had passed out of physical life in the catastrophe of the Deluge, persons who most assuredly had perished on account of their transgression of the Law. For further study of this subject I would refer the reader to the works of two orthodox divines, Farrar's *Eternal Hope* and Plumptre's *Spirits in Prison*.*

The transgression of which Jesus speaks is the transgression of the Law of the I AM in ourselves, the nonrecognition of the fact that we are the image and likeness of God. This is the old original

*Farrar: see footnote, p. 47; Edward Hayes Plumptre (1821–1891)—*Ed.*

sin of Eve. It is the belief in Evil as a substantive self-originating power. We believe ourselves under the control of all sorts of evils having their climax in Death; but whence does the evil get its power? Not from God, for no diminution of Life can come from the Fountain of Life. And if not from God, then from where else? God is the ONLY BEING—that is the teaching of the First Commandment—and therefore whatever is, is some mode of God; and if this be so, then however evil may have *relative* existence, it can have no *substantive* existence of its own. It is not a Living Originating Power. God, the Good, alone is *that*; and it is for this reason that in the doctrine of THE ONE and in the statement of the I AM is the foundation of eternal *individual* Life and Liberty.

So then the transgression is in supposing that there is, or can be, any Living Originating Power outside the I AM. Let us once see that this is impossible, and it follows that evil has no more dominion over us and we are free. But so long as we limit the I AM in ourselves to the narrow boundaries of the relative and conditioned and do not realize that, personified in ourselves, it must by its very nature still be as unfettered as when acting in the first creation of the universe, we shall never pass beyond the Law of Death, which we thus impose upon ourselves.

In this way, then, Jesus proved himself to be the Prophet of whom Moses had spoken. He made the recognition of the I AM the sole foundation of his work; in other words, He placed before men the same radical and ultimate conception of Being that Moses had done. But with a difference. Moses elaborated this conception from the standpoint of the Universal; Jesus elaborated it from that of the Individual. The work of Moses must necessarily precede that of Jesus, for if the Universal Mind is not in some measure apprehended first, the individual mind cannot be apprehended as its image and reflection.

But it takes the teaching both of Moses and Jesus to make the complete teaching, for each is the complement to the other, and it is for this reason that Jesus said he came not to destroy the Law but to fulfil. Jesus took up the work where Moses left it off and expanded Moses' initial conception, of a people founded on the recognition of the unity of God, into its proper outcome of the conception of a people founded on the recognition of the unity of Man as the expression of the Unity of God.

How can we doubt that this latter conception also was in the mind of Moses? Had it not been, he would not have spoken of the Prophet like unto himself that should come hereafter. But he saw the ages during which his great idea must germinate within the limits of a single nationality before it could expand to humanity at large; and therefore before Jesus could gather into one the "People of the I AM" from every nation under heaven, it was necessary that one exclusive nation should be the official custodians of the great secret and mature it till the time was ripe for the formation of that great international nationality which is only now beginning to show forth its earliest blossoms.

CHAPTER 5

The Mission of Jesus

Hitherto, our interpretation of the Bible has worked along the line of great Universal Laws naturally inherent in the constitution of Man and thus applicable to all men alike; but now we must turn to that other line of an Exclusive Selection to which I referred in the opening chapter. This is not an arbitrary selection—for that would contradict the very conception of unchangeable Universal Law on which the whole Bible is founded—but it is a process of "natural selection" arising out of the Law itself and results not from any change in the Law, but from the attainment of an exalted realization of what the Law really is.

The first suggestion of this process of separation is contained in the promise that the deliverance of the race should come through "the Seed of the Woman," for in contradistinction to this "Seed" there is the seed of the Serpent; "I will put enmity between thy seed and her seed." Again we see the process of selection coming out in the preference given to the offering of Abel over that of Cain, and again the selection is repeated in the intimation that Seth took the place of Abel, while it is to be remarked that the New Testament genealogy traces the ancestry of Jesus to Seth; so that the line of Seth is clearly indicated as carrying on the selection originally made in favor of Abel. In this line we find Noah, who, with his family, was alone excepted from the universal overthrow of the Deluge; and many centuries later we find one man, Abraham, selected by means of a special covenant to be the progenitor of a chosen race from which in process of time the Messiah, the Promised Seed of the Woman, was to be born.

Now was there in these things any arbitrary selection? After due consideration, we shall find that there was not and that they arose out of the perfectly natural operation of mental laws working on the higher levels of Individualism, and the indications of this operation are given in the story of Cain and Abel. Abel was a keeper of sheep and Cain was a tiller of the earth, and if the reader will bear in mind what I have said regarding the symbolic character of Bible personages and the metaphorical use of words, the meaning of the story will become clear.

There is a great difference between animal and

vegetable life: the one is cold and devoid of any apparent element of volition, the other is full of warmth and adumbrates the quality of Will; so that as symbols, the animal represents the emotional qualities in Man, while the vegetable, following a mere law of sequence without the exercise of individual choice, more fitly represents the purely logical processes of reasoning. Now we all know that the first spring of action in any chain of cause and effect which we set going starts with some emotion, some manner of *feeling*, and not with a mere argument. Argument, a reasoning process, may cause us to change the standpoint of our feeling and to conceive that as desirable which at first we did not consider so; but at the end it is the recognition of a desire which is the one and only spring of action. It is, therefore, the feelings and desires that give the true key to our life, and not mere logical statements; and so if the feelings and desires are going in the right direction, we may be very sure that the logic will not be wrong in its conclusions, even though it may be blundering in its method. Take care of the heart, and the head will take care of itself.

This, then, is the meaning of the story of Cain and Abel. If we realize that the Universal Mind, as the All-pervading undistributed Creative Power, must be subjective mind, we shall see that it can only respond in accordance with the Law of subjective mind; that is to say, its relation to the individual mind must always be in exact correspondence to what the individual mind conceives of it. This is unequivocally stated in a passage which is twice repeated in Scripture: "With the pure Thou wilt show Thyself pure; and with the froward Thou wilt show Thyself froward" (Psalm 18:26, and 2 Sam. 22:27), where the context makes it clear that these words are addressed to the Divine Being. If, therefore, we grasp this Law of Correspondence, we shall see that the only conception of the Divine Mind which will really vivify our souls with living and life-giving power is to realize it not merely as a tremendous force to be mapped out intellectually according to its successive stages of sequence—though it is this also—but above all things as the Universal Heart with which our own must beat in sympathetic vibration if we would attain the true development of that power the possession of which constitutes "the glorious liberty of the sons of God."

In all our operations we must always remember that the Creative Power is a process of *feeling* and not of reasoning. Reasoning analyzes and dissects; feeling evolves and builds up. The relation between them is that reasoning explains *how* it is that feeling has this power; and the more plainly we see *why* it should be so, the more completely we are delivered from those negative feelings which act destructively by the same law by which affirmative feelings work constructively.

The first requisite, therefore, for drawing to ourselves that creative action of the Universal Spirit, which alone can set us free from the bondage of Limitation, is to call up its response on the side of feeling; and unless this be done first, no amount of argument, mere intellectuality, can have the desired effect, and this is what is symbolically represented in the statement that God accepted Abel's offering and rejected Cain's. It is the veiled statement of the truth that the action of the intellect alone, however powerful, is not sufficient to move the Creative Power. This does not in the least mean that the intellectual process is hurtful in itself or unacceptable before God, but it must come in its proper order as joining with feeling instead of taking its place. When a mere cold ratiocination is substituted for hearty warmth of volition, then Abel is symbolically slain by Cain.

But the allegory goes further. It tells us that the particular animal which Abel offered in sacrifice was the sheep; and from this point onward we find the metaphor of the shepherd and the sheep recurring throughout Scripture, and the reason is that the relation between the Shepherd and the Sheep is peculiarly one of Guidance and Protection. Now this brings us to the point which we may call the "Severance of the Way." When we realize the Unity of the I AM—the identity, that is, of the Self-recognizing Principle in the Universal and in the Individual—we may form three conceptions of it: one according to which the Universal I AM is reduced to a mere unconscious force, which the individual mind can manipulate without any sort of responsibility; another, the converse of this, in which Volition remains entirely on the side of the Universal Mind, and the individual becomes a mere automaton; and the third, in which each phase of Mind is the reciprocal of the other, and consequently the inceptive action may commence on either side.

Now it is this *reciprocal* action that the Bible all along puts before us as the true Way. From the centre of his own smaller circle of perception the individual is free to make any selection that he will, and if he acts from a clear recognition of the true relations of things, the first use he will make of this power will be to guard himself against any possible misuse of it by recognizing that his own circle revolves within the greater circle of that Whole of which he is an infinitesimal part; and therefore he will always seek to conform his individual action to the movement of the Universal Spirit.

His sense of the *Wholeness* of that Universal Life which finds Individual centre in himself, and his consciousness of his identity with it, will lead him to see that there must be, above his own individual view of things derived from a merely partial knowledge, a higher and more far-seeing Wisdom which, because it is the Life-in-itself, cannot be in any way adverse to him; and he will therefore seek to maintain such a mental attitude as will draw towards himself the response of the Universal Mind as a Power of unfailing Guidance, Provision, and Protection. But to do this means the curbing of that self-will which is guided only by the narrow perception of expediency derived from past experiences; in other words, it requires us to act from trust in the Universal Mind, thus investing it with a Personal character, rather than from calculations based on our own objective view, which is necessarily limited to secondary causes. In a word, we must learn to walk by faith and not by sight.

Now the institution of Sacrifice is the most effective way for impressing this mental attitude. Viewed merely superficially, it implies the desire of the worshipper to submit himself to the Divine Guidance by reconciliation through a propitiatory offering, and thus the required mental attitude is maintained. If we see that the blood of bulls and goats and the ashes of a heifer can have no power in themselves to effect reconciliation, and yet cannot see any more intelligible reason, then, if we will to accept the principle of sacrifice in the light of a mere mystery, we hereby still submit our individual will to the conception of a Higher Guidance, and so in this view also the desired mental attitude is maintained.

And at last when we reach the point where we see that the Universal Mind, which is also the Universal LAW, cannot have a retrospective vindictive character any more than any of the Laws of Nature which emanate from it, we see that the true sacrifice is the willingness to give up smaller personal aims for the purpose of bringing into concrete manifestation those great principles of universal harmony which are the foundations of the Kingdom of God; and when we reach this point, we see the philosophical reasons why the maintenance of this attitude of the individual towards the Universal Mind is the one and only basis on which the individuality can expand or, indeed, continue to exist at all.

It is in correspondence with these three stages that the Bible first puts before us the patriarchal and Levitical sacrifices, next explains these as symbols of the Great Sacrifice of the Suffering Messiah, and finally tells us that God does not require the death of any victim and that the true offering is that of the heart and will; and so the Psalms sum up the whole matter by saying, "Sacrifice and burnt-offering thou wouldest not," and instead of these, "Lo, I come to do Thy will, O my God; yea, Thy law is within my heart."

But the idea of Sacrifice has the idea of Covenant for its correlative. If the acceptance of the principle of Sacrifice brings the worshipper into a peculiarly close relation to the Divine Mind, it equally brings the Divine Mind into a peculiarly close relation to the worshipper; and since the Divine Mind is the Life-in-itself, the very Essence-of-Being which is the *root* of all conscious individuality, this identification of the Divine with the Individual results in his continual expansion, or, to use the Master's words, in his having Life and having it more abundantly; and consequently, his powers steadily increase, and he is led by the most unlooked-for sequences of cause and effect into continually improving conditions which enable him to do more and more effectual work, so as to make him a centre of power, not only to himself, but to all with whom he comes in contact.

This continual progress is the result of the natural Law of the relation between himself and the Universal Mind when he does not invert its action, and because it works with the same unchangeableness as all other Natural Laws, it constitutes an Everlasting Covenant which can no more be broken than those astronomical laws which keep the planets in their orbits, the smallest infraction of which would destroy the entire cosmic system; and it is for this reason that we find in the Bible such frequent allusions to the Laws of Nature as typical of the certainty of the relation between God and his people. "Gather My saints [separated ones] together unto Me; those that have made a covenant with me by sacrifice" (Psalm 50:5); the two principles of Sacrifice and Covenant rightly understood will always be found to go hand in hand.

The idea of Guidance and Protection which is thus set forth recurs throughout the Bible under the emblem of the Shepherd and the Sheep, and it is in a peculiar manner appropriated to "the People of the I AM": "From thence is the Shepherd, the Stone of Israel" (Gen. 49:24); "Give ear, O Shepherd of Israel, Thou that leadest Joseph like a flock" (Psalm 80:1); "The Lord is My Shepherd; I shall not want" (Psalm 23:1); "I am the Good Shepherd"; and similarly in many other passages.

If, then, this conception of the Shepherd and the Sheep represents the mental attitude of "Israel," we may reasonably expect it to be precisely opposite to all that is symbolically meant by "Egypt." If "Israel" takes for its Stone of Foundation the principle of Guidance by the Supreme Power, then "Egypt" must base itself on the contrary principle of making its own choice without any guidance—that is to say, determined self-will. And hence we find it written that "every Shepherd is an abomination to the Egyptians" (Gen. 46:34).

Now it is a very remarkable thing that tradition points to the Great Pyramid as having been erected by a "Shepherd" power which dominated Egypt, not by force of arms, but by a mysterious influence, which, although they detested it, the Egyptians found it impossible to resist. These "Shepherds" built the Great Pyramid and then, having accomplished their work, returned to the land from whence they came. So says the tradition. The Pyramid remains to this day, and the researches of modern science show that it is a monumental statement of all the great measures of the cosmic system wrought out with an accuracy which can only be accounted for by more than human knowledge.

And where should we find this knowledge except in the Universal Mind, of which the cosmic system is the visible manifestation? If, as it appears to me, that mind is primarily subconscious, then, by the general law of relation between subjective and objective mind, it could reproduce its inherent knowledge of all cosmic facts in any individual mind that had systematically trained itself into sympathy with the Universal Mind in that particular direction. But such training is impossible unless the individual mind first recognizes the Universal Mind as an Intelligence capable of giving the highest instruction, and to which, therefore, the individual mind is bound to look for guidance.

We must carefully avoid the mistake of supposing that *sub*consciousness means *un*consciousness. That idea is clearly negatived by the fact of hypnotism. Whatever unconsciousness there may be is on the part of the objective mind, which is unconscious of the action of the subjective mind. But a careful study of the subject shows that subjective mind, so far from knowing less than the objective mind, knows infinitely more; and if this be true of the individual subjective mind, how much more must it be true of the Universal Subjective Mind, of which all individual consciousness is a particular mode of manifestation?

For these reasons, the only people who could build such a monument as a Great Pyramid must be those who realized the principles of Divine Guidance or the Power which is set forth under the emblem of the Shepherd and the Sheep; and therefore we can see how it is that tradition associates the building of the Pyramid with a Shepherd Power.

Nor is this all. Having first demonstrated its trustworthiness by the refined accuracy of its astronomical and geodetic measurements, the Pyramid challenges our attention with a series of time-measurements, all of which were prophetic at the date of its erection, and some of which have already become historic, while the period of others is now rapidly running out. The central point of these time-measurements is the date of the birth of Christ, and if we think of Him in His character of "the Good Shepherd," we have yet another testimony to the supreme importance which Scripture attaches to the relation between the Shepherd and the Sheep. For the Great Pyramid is a Bible in stone, and there can be no doubt that it is this marvel of the ages which is referred to in the nineteenth chapter of Isaiah, where it says, "In that day there shall be an altar to the Lord in the midst of the land of Egypt."

And so we find that the central fact to which the Great Pyramid leads up is the coming of "the Good Shepherd"; and Jesus explains the reason for this title in the fact that "the Good Shepherd giveth His life for the Sheep." That is what distinguishes Him from the hireling who is not a true shepherd; so that here we find ourselves back again at the idea of Sacrifice, only now it is not the Sheep that are sacrificed, but the Shepherd. Could anything be plainer? The sacrifice is not an offering of blood to a sanguinary Deity, but it is the Chief Shepherd sacrificing Himself *to the necessities of the case*.

And what are the necessities of the case? The student of Mental Science should see here the grandest application of the Law of Suggestion in a supreme act of self-devotion logically proceeding from the knowledge of the fundamental truths regarding Subjective and Objective Mind. Jesus stands before us as the Grand Master of Mental Science. It is written that "He knew what was in man," and in His mission we have the practical fruits of that knowledge.

The Great Sacrifice is also the Great Suggestion. If we realize that the Creative Power of our Thought is the root from which all our experiences, whether subjective or objective, arise, we shall see that everything depends on the nature of the suggestions which give color to our Thought. If from our consciousness of guilt they are suggestions of retribution, then, in accordance with the predominating tone of our Thought, we shall externalize the evil that we fear; and if we carry this terrible suggestion with us through the gate of death into that other life which is purely subjective, then assuredly it will work itself out in our realizations, and so we must continue to suffer until we believe that we have paid the uttermost farthing. This is not a judicial sentence, but the inexorable working of Natural Law. But if we can find a counter-suggestion of such paramount magnitude as to obliterate all sense of liability to punishment, then, by the same Law, our fears are removed; and whether in the body or out of the body, we rejoice in the sense of pardon and reconciliation to our Father which is in heaven.

Now we can well imagine that one who has attained the supreme knowledge of all Laws, and as a consequence has developed the powers which that knowledge must necessarily carry with it, would find in the conveying of such an incalculably valuable suggestion to the race an object worthy of his exalted capacities. For such a one, ordinary ambitions would have no meaning; he has already left them far behind. But if he elects to devote himself to this great work, he must count the cost, for nothing short of delivering himself to death can accomplish it. The Master said, "Greater love hath no man than this, that a man lay down his life for his friends," and if the Law of Suggestion was to be employed in such a way as to appeal to the whole race, it could only be by so deeply impressing them with the realization of the Divine Love that all fear should be forever cast out; therefore the suggestion must be that of a Love which nothing can exceed, and so it must consist in him who undertakes the mission giving himself to Voluntary Death.

For herein is the difference between the crucifixion of Jesus and those thousands of other crucifixions which disgraced the annals of Rome: it was entirely voluntary. This also places it above all other acts of heroism. Many have died for the sake of others, but to them death was a necessity, and their devotion consisted in accepting it when and how they did. But with Jesus the case was entirely different. He was beyond the necessity of death, and no man could take His life from Him; He Himself had power to lay it down and to take it up again (John 10:17), but He was under no compulsion to do so; therefore His yielding Himself to a death of excruciating agony was the master-stroke of Love and the supreme practical application of Mental Science.

When He said, "It is finished," He had accomplished a work which is aptly represented by The Cubical Stone, which is The Figure of the New Jerusalem, of which it is written that "the length, and the breadth, and the height thereof are equal."* For turn it which way you will, it still always serves its great purpose of impressing the suggestions of superlative Love which can be trusted to the uttermost. Even the crude conception of the Father's "justice" being satisfied by the sacrifice of "the Son," however faulty both as Law and as Theology, in no way misses the mark from the metaphysical standpoint of Suggestion; and those who have not yet got beyond this stage in their conception of the Divine Being receive the assurance of the Divine Love towards themselves as completely as those who are able to grasp most clearly the sequence of cause and effect really involved; and for these latter it resolves itself into the simple argument *a fortiori*† that if the Universal Spirit could thus inspire one to die for us who was already beyond the necessity of death, then It cannot be less loving in the bulk than it has shown Itself in the sample.

It is an axiom that the Universal cannot act on the plane of the Particular except by becoming individualized upon that plane, and therefore we may argue that so far as it was possible for the Universal Spirit to give Itself to death for us, It did so in the person of Jesus Christ; and so we may say that

*Revelation 21:16—*Ed.*
†In the sense "with still greater reason"—*Ed.*

to all intents and purposes God died for us upon the Cross to prove to us the Love of God.

Let us, then, no longer doubt the fact of this Love, but, realizing it to the full, let us make the Cross of Christ not the mysterious end of an unintelligent religion, but the beginning of a bright, practical, and glorious New Life, taking for our starting-point the apostolic words, "there is now no condemnation to them that are in Christ Jesus." We have now *consciously* left all condemnation behind us, and we set forward on our New Life with the self-obvious maxim that "if God be for us, who can be against us?" We may meet with opposition, but there is with us a Power and an Intelligence which no opposition can overcome, and so we become "more than conquerors through Him that loved us" (Rom. 8:37).

This is the nature of the Great Suggestion wrought out by Jesus; so that here again we find that the acceptance of the Great Sacrifice gives rise to the consciousness of a peculiarly close and endearing relation between the Individual and the Universal Mind, which may well be described as an Everlasting Covenant because it is founded not on any favoritism on the part of God, neither on any deeds of merit on the part of Man, but on the accurate working of Universal Law when realized in the higher manifestations of Individualism; and so it is truly written, "by His *Knowledge* shall My righteous servant justify many." Thus it is that Jesus completes the work of Moses in building up into a peculiar people, a chosen generation, "the People of the I AM" (1 Peter 2:9).

It was this conception of themselves as a chosen nation, separate from all others and united to God by a special covenant based upon sacrifice, that did in effect operate to produce the reality of this ideal in the people of Israel. Here again we see the Law of Suggestion at work. All their institutions, whether religious or political, were based upon the assumption of a covenant with Abraham forever ratified to his descendants, and centering round the promised Messiah; and so, whether looking at the past, the present, or the future, an Israelite was perpetually met by the most powerful suggestion of his peculiar position in the Divine favor.

If we recognize in Abraham one whose deep realization of the truth concerning the promised "Seed" had specially placed him in touch with the Universal Mind in that particular direction, we may naturally suppose a special illumination on this subject which would lead him to impress this idea upon his son Isaac as the foundation-fact of his life; and so from generation to generation, the supreme realization to all his descendants would be that of their covenant relation to God. And besides the impression conveyed by personal teaching, the law of heredity would cause each member of this race to be born with a prenatal subjective consciousness of this great Suggestion, which would carry its effect into the building up of his life, quite independently of any objectively conscious knowledge of the subject. This involves intricate psychological problems which I cannot stop to discuss here, but all New Thought readers are sufficiently acquainted with the potency of "race-beliefs" to realize how powerful a factor this subjective transmission of a hereditary suggestion would be in forming "the people of the I AM."

And there is yet another aspect of this subject which is of peculiar interest to the British and American nations, into which, however, I shall not enter in this book; but it will be sufficient for me to say that when a suggestion has once been implanted by the Divine Mind, as the Bible tells us that God did to Abraham in the most emphatic manner, taking oath by His own Being because He could swear by none greater (Heb. 6:13), that suggestion is bound to grow to the most magnificent fulfillment: "My word that goeth forth out of My mouth shall not return unto Me void, but shall accomplish that which I please, and it shall prosper in the thing whereunto I sent it" (Isaiah 55:11).

For the reasons which I have now endeavored to explain, the principle of "the Shepherd" is "the Stone of Israel"; it is that great ideal by which the nationality of the "People of the I AM" coheres, and it is, therefore, at once the Foundation Stone and the Crowning Stone of the whole edifice. To those who cannot realize the great universal truths which are summed up in the twofold ideal of Sacrifice and Covenant, it must always be the Stone of stumbling and the Rock of offence; but to "the People of the I AM," whether individually or collectively, it must forever be "the Stone of Israel" and "the Rock of our Salvation." To lay in Zion this Chief Corner Stone was the mission of Jesus Christ.

CHAPTER 6

The Building of the Temple

In our study of the Bible, we must always remember that what it is seeking to teach us is the knowledge of the grand universal principles which are at the root of all modes of living activity, whether in that world of enviroment which we commonly speak of as Nature, or in those human relations which we call the World of Man, or in those innermost springs of being which we speak of as the Divine World. The Bible is throughout dealing with those three factors, which I have spoken of in the commencement of this book as "God," "Man," and "the Universe," and is explaining the Law of Evolution by which "God" or Universal Undifferentiated Spirit continually passes into more and more perfect forms of Self-expression culminating in Perfected Man.

However deep the mysteries we may encounter, there is nothing unnatural anywhere. Everything has its place in the due order of the Great Whole.

A mistaken conception of this Order may lead us to invert it, and by so doing we provide those negative conditions whose presence calls forth the Power of the Negative with all its disastrous consequences; but even this inverted action is perfectly natural, for it is all according to recognizable Law, whether on the side of calculation or of feeling.

These Laws of the universe, whether within or around us, are always the same, and the only question is whether through our ignorance we shall use them in that inverted sense which sums them all up in the Law of Death, or in that true and harmonious order which sums them up in the Law of Life. These are the things which under a variety of figures the Bible presents to us, and it is for us by reverent, yet intelligent, inquiry to penetrate the successive veils which hide them from the eyes of those who will not take the trouble to investigate for themselves. It is this Grand Order of the Universe that is symbolized by Solomon's Temple.

We have seen that it was the mission of Moses to mould into definite form the material which ages of unnoticed growth had prepared, to consolidate into national being "the People of the I AM," and to lead them out of Egypt. This work, with which the truly national history of Israel commenced, had its completion in the reign of Solomon, when all enemies had been extirpated from the Promised

Land, and the state founded by Moses out of wandering tribes had culminated in a powerful monarchy, ruled over by a king whose name has ever since become both in East and West the synonym for the supreme attainment of wisdom, power, and glory.

If the purpose of Moses had been only that of a national lawgiver and the founder of a political state, a Lycurgus* or a Rollo,† it would have found its perfect attainment in the reign of Solomon; but Moses had a far grander end in view, and looking down the long vista of the ages, he saw not Solomon but the Carpenter, who said, "a greater than Solomon is here."‡ And the way for the Carpenter could only be prepared by that long period of decadence which set in with the first days of Solomon's successor. "The People of the I AM" are concealed among all nations and must be brought forth by the Prophet, who should realize the work of Moses not only in a national, but also in a universal, significance.

These are the three typical figures of Hebrew history; the beginning, the middle, and the end—

*9th century B.C. Spartan lawgiver—*Ed.*

†(ca. A.D. 860–932) Scandinavian wanderer and founder of the duchy of Normandy—*Ed.*

‡Matt. 12:42; Luke 11:31—*Ed.*

Moses, Solomon, Jesus; and the three are distinguished by one common characteristic: they are all Builders of the Temple. Moses erected the tabernacle, that portable temple which accompanied the Israelites in their journeyings. Solomon reproduced it in an edifice of wood and stone fixed firmly upon its rocky foundation. Jesus said, "Destroy this temple, and in three days I will raise it up again"; but "He spake of the temple of His body."

Thus they stand before us the Three Great Builders, each building with a perfect knowledge according to a Divine pattern; and if the Divine is that in which there is no variableness nor shadow of turning,* how can we suppose that the pattern was other than one and the same? We may, therefore, expect to find in the work of the Three Builders the same *principles*, however differently expressed; for they each in different ways proclaimed the same all-embracing truth that God, Man, and the Universe, however varied may be the multiplicity of outward forms, are ONE.

St. Paul gives us an important key to the interpretation of Scripture when he tells us that its leading characters also represent great universal principles, and this is preeminently the case with

*James 1:17—*Ed.*

Solomon. His name, in common with the names Salem and Jerusalem, is derived from a word signifying Wholeness (Sálim, the Whole), and therefore means the man who has realized "the Wholeness," or in other words the Universal Unity. This is the secret of his greatness.

He who has found the Unity of the Whole has obtained "the Key of Knowledge," and it is now in his power to enter intelligently upon the study of his own being and of the relations which arise out of it, and to help others as he himself advances into greater light. This is the man who is able to become a Builder.

But such a man cannot come of any parentage; he must be the "Son of David"; and it was to test their knowledge in this respect that the Master posed the carping scribes with the question as to how the Son of David could also be his Lord. As rulers in Israel, they should have known these things and instructed the people in them, but they would not come, as did Nicodemus, to Him who would teach them; and so, like Hiram, the architect of Solomon's Temple, the Master was murdered by those who should have been His scholars and helpers.

The Builder of the Temple, then, must be "the Son of David"; and again we find that much of the significance of this saying is concealed in the names. David is the English form of the Oriental "Daud," which means "Beloved," and the Builder is therefore the Son of the Beloved. David is called in Scripture "the man after God's own heart," a description exactly answering to the name; and we therefore find that Solomon the Builder is the son of the man who has entered into that reciprocal relation with "God," or the Universal Spirit, which can only be described as Love.

To define what is primarily *feeling* is to attempt the impossible; but the essence of the feeling consists in the recognition of such a reciprocity of nature that each supplies what the other wants, and that neither is complete without the other. In the last analysis, the reason for this feeling is to be discovered in the relation of the Individual to the Universal Mind as each being the necessary correlative of the other, and it is the recognition of this truth that makes David the father of Solomon.

When this recognition by the individual mind of its own nature and of its relation to the Universal Mind takes place, it gives birth to a new being in the man; for he now finds not that he has ceased to be the self he was before, but that that self includes a far greater self, which is none other than the reproduction of the Universal Self in his individual consciousness. Thenceforward he works more and more *of set purpose* by means of this greater self, the self within the self, as he grows into fuller understanding of the Law by which this greater self has become developed within him.

He learns that it is this greater self within the self that is the true Builder, because it is none other than the reproduction of the Infinite Creative Power of the Universe. He realizes that the working of this power must always be a continual building up. It is the Universal Life-Principle, and to suppose *that* to have any other action than continual expansion into more and more perfect forms of self-expression would be to suppose it acting in contradiction of its own nature, which, whether on the colossal scale of a solar system or on the miniature one of a man, must be that of a self-inherent activity which is forever building up.

When anyone is thus intellectually enlightened, he has reached that stage of development which is signified by the name David: he is "beloved"—that is to say, he is exercising a specific individual *attraction* towards the Spirit in its universal and undifferentiated mode.

We are here dealing with the Principle of Evolution in its highest phases, and if we keep this in mind, it becomes clear that the intellectual man, who perceives this, is himself the evolving principle manifesting at that stage where it becomes an individuality capable of understanding its own identity with the Spiritual Force which, by Self-evolution, produces all things. He thus realizes himself to be the Reciprocal of the Universal Mind, which is the Divine Spirit, and he sees that his reciprocity consists in Evolution having reached in him the point where that factor is developed which cannot have a place in the Universal Mind *as such*, but without which the continuation of Evolution in its higher phases is impossible—the factor, namely, of *individual* will.

We lose the key to the whole teaching of the Bible if we lose sight of the truth that the Universal cannot, as such, initiate a course of action on the plane of the particular. It can do so only by becoming the individual, which is precisely the production of the intellectually enlightened man we are speaking about. The failure to see this very obvious Law is the root of all the theological discordances that have retarded the work of true religion to the present time, and therefore the sooner we see through the error, the better.

Anyone who has advanced to the perception of this Law necessarily becomes a centre of attraction to Undifferentiated Spirit in its highest modes, the modes of Intelligence and Feeling, as well as in its lower modes of Vital Energy. This results from the very nature of the evolutionary hypothesis. All creation commences with the primary movement of the Spirit, and since the Spirit is Life-in-itself, this movement must be forever going on.

To take an analogy from chemistry, it is perpetually in the nascent state—that is, continually pressing forward to find the most suitable affinities with which to coalesce into self-expresison. This is exactly what Jesus said to the woman of Samaria: "The Father [Universal Spirit] *seeketh* such to worship Him"; and it is because of this mutual attraction between the individual mind that has come to the knowledge of its own true nature and the Universal Mind, that the person who is thus enlightened is called "the Beloved"; he is beginning to understand what is meant by man being the image of God and to grasp the significance of the old-world saying that "Spirit is the power that knows itself."

As this intellectual comprehension of the great truth matures, it gives rise to the recognition of an interior power which is something beyond the intellect but yet not independent of it, something regarding which we can make intellectual statements that clear the way for its recognition, but which is itself a Living Power and not a mere statement about such a power.

It may seem a truism to say that no statement about a thing *is* the thing, yet we are apt to miss this in practice. The Master pointed this out very clearly when He said to the Jews, "Search the Scriptures, for in them ye *think* ye have everlasting life, and they are they which testify of Me." "You make a mistake," He said in effect, "by supposing that the reading of a book can in itself confer Life. What your Scriptures do is to make statements regarding that which I am. Realize what those statements mean, and then you will see in Me the Living Example of the Living Truth; and seeing this, you will seek for the development of the same thing in yourselves. The disciple, when he is perfected, shall be as his Master."

The Building-Power is that innermost spiritual faculty which is the reproduction in the individual of the same Universal Building-Power by which the whole creation exists, and the purpose of intellectual statements regarding it is to remove mental obstacles and to induce the mental state which will enable this supreme innermost power to work in accordance with conscious selection on the part of the individual. It is the same power which has brought the race up to where it is, and which has evolved the individual as part of the race.

All further evolution must result from the conscious employment of the Evolutionary Law by the intelligence of the individual himself. Now it is this recognized innermost creative power that is signified by Solomon—it must be preceded by the purified and enlightened intellect—and therefore it is called the Son of David and becomes the Builder of the Temple. For the Master's statement shows that, in its true significance, the Temple is that of Man's individuality; and if this is so with the individual, equally it must be so in the totality of manifested being, and thus it is also true that the whole universe is none other than the Temple of the Living God.

This great truth of the Divine Presence is what the instructed builders sought to symbolize in Solomon's Temple, whether that Presence be considered on the scale of the universe or of an individual man. If the Universal Divine Presence is a fact, then the Individual Divine Presence is a fact also, because the individual is included in the universal; it is the working of the general Law in a particular instance, and thus we are brought to one of the great statements of the ancient wisdom, that Man is the Microcosm—that is to say, the reproduction of all the principles which give rise to the manifestation of the universe, or the Macrocosm; and therefore, to serve its proper emblematical purpose, the Temple must represent both the Macrocosm and the Microcosm.

It would be far too elaborate a work, for the present volume, to enter in detail into the symbolical statements of both physical and supraphysical nature contained first in the Tabernacle and afterwards in the Temple; but as the Universal Mind inspired the builders of the Pyramid with the correct knowledge of the cosmic measures, so the Bible tells us that Moses was inspired to produce in the Tabernacle the symbolic representation of great universal truths; he was bidden to make all things accurately according to the pattern showed him in the Mount, and the same truths received a more permanent symbolization in Solomon's Temple.

An excellent example of this symbolism is afforded by the two pillars set up by Solomon at the entrance to the Temple: the one on the right hand, called Jachin, and the one on the left, called Boaz (1 Kings 7:21). They seemed to have had no structural connection with the building but merely to have stood at its entrance for the purpose of bearing these symbolic names. What, then, do they signify? The English J often stands for the Oriental Y, and the name Jachin is therefore Yakhin, which is an intensified form of the word Yak or ONE, thus signifying first the principle of Unity as the Foundation of all things, and then the Mathematical element throughout the universe, since all numbers are evolved from the ONE, and under certain methods of treatment will always resolve themselves again into it.

But the Mathematical element is the element of

Measurement, Proportion, and Relation. It is not the Living Life, but only the recognition of the proportional adjustments which the Life gives rise to. To balance the Mathematical element we require the Vital element, and this element finds its most perfect expression in that wonderful complex of Thought, Feeling, and Volition which we call Personality. The pillar Jachin is therefore balanced by the pillar Boaz, a name connected with the root of the word "awaz" or Voice.*

Speech is the distinguishing characteristic of Personality. To clothe a conception in adequate language is to give it definition and thus make it clear to ourselves and to others. A distinct statement of our idea is the first step in the operation of consciously building it up into concrete existence, and therefore we find that in all the great religions of the race, the Divine Creative Power is spoken of as "the Word."

Let us get away from all confused mysticism regarding this term. The formulated Word is the expression of a definite Purpose, and therefore it stands for the action of Intelligent Volition; and it is as showing the place which this factor holds in the evolutionary process that the pillar Boaz stands

*See "Jachin and Boaz," in *Collected Essays of Thomas Troward* (DeVorss & Co.), pp. 150–53.—*Ed.*

opposite the pillar Jachin as its necessary complement and equilibration. The union of the two signifies Intelligent Purpose working by means of Necessary Law, and the only way of entering into "the Temple," whether of the cosmos or of the individual, is by passing between these Two Pillars of the Universe and realizing the combined action of Law and Volition.

This is the Narrow Way that leads us into the building not made with hands,* within which all the mysteries shall be unfolded before us in a regular order and succession. He who climbs up some other way is a thief and a robber and brings punishment upon himself as the natural effect of his own rashness; for, knowing nothing of the *true* Order of the Inner Life, he plunges prematurely into the midst of things of whose real nature he is ignorant, and sooner or later learns to his cost the truth of the Scriptural warning "whoso breaketh an hedge, a serpent shall bite him" (Eccl. 10:8).

We may not enter the Temple save by passing between the pillars, and we cannot pass between them till we can tell their meaning. It is the purpose of the Bible to give us the Key to this Knowledge. It is not the only instruction it has to give, but it is its initial course, and when this has been mastered,

*2 Corinthians 5:1—*Ed.*

it will open out deeper things, the inner secrets of the sanctuary. But the first thing is to pass between Jachin and Boaz, and then the Divine Interpreter will meet us on the threshold and will unfold the mysteries of the Temple in their due order, so that as each one is opened to us in succession, we are prepared for its reception and thus need fear no danger, because at each step we always know that we are dealing with and have attained the spiritual, intellectual, and physical development qualifying us to employ each new revelation in the right way.

For the opening of the inner mysteries is not for the gratification of mere idle curiosity; it is for the increasing of our Livingness; and the highest quality of Livingness is Life-givingness; and every measure of Live-givingness, be it only the giving of a cup of cold water,* means *use* of the powers and knowledge which we possess. The Temple instruction is therefore intended to qualify us as *workers*, and the value to ourselves of what we receive within is seen in the measure of intelligence and love with which we transmute our Temple gold into the current coin of daily life.

The building-up process is that of Evolution, whether in the material world or in the human individuality or in the race as a whole, and the

*Matthew 10:42—*Ed.*

Bible presents the analogy to us very forcibly under the metaphor of "the Stone." Speaking of the rejection of His own teaching, the Master said, "What is this, then, that is written, 'The Stone which the builders rejected, the same is become the head of the corner'?" referring to the 118th Psalm (Luke 20:17). A careful perusal of the Master's history as given in the Gospel will show us very clearly what "the Stone" is; it is the material out of which the Temple of the Spirit is to be built up, which we now see is nothing else than Perfected Humanity.

Each individual is a temple himself, as St. Paul tells us, and at the same time a single stone in the construction of the Great Temple which is the regenerated race, that "People of the I AM" which was inaugurated when Moses first pitched the tabernacle in the wilderness. But the process must always be an individual one, for a nation is nothing but an aggregation of individuals, and therefore in considering the metaphor of "the Stone" as applied to the individual, we shall realize its wider application also.

Now the Master was executed on the charge of blasphemy for asserting the identity of His own nature with that of God. The subjection of the Jews to the Roman rule placed the power of life and death in the hands of a tribunal which could not take cognizance of such an offence—"Take ye Him and judge Him according to *your* law," said Pilate, when the charge of blasphemy was preferred before him; and in order to bring Him to execution it became necessary to substitute for the original charge of blasphemy one of high treason, so as to bring it within the jurisdiction of the court. "Whosoever maketh himself a king speaketh against Caesar"—and so the inscription fastened to the cross was "Jesus of Nazareth, the King of the Jews." But the true reason why He was hunted to death was expressed by the scribes, who mocked the Sufferer with the words "He trusted in God; let Him deliver Him now if He will have Him, for He said, 'I am the Son of God'."

The teaching of Jesus was the inversion of all that was taught by the official priesthood. Their whole teaching rested on the hypothesis that God and Man are absolutely distinct *in nature*, thus directly contradicting the earliest statement of their own Scriptures regarding Man, that he is the image and likeness of God. As a consequence of this false assumption, they supposed that the whole Mosaic Law and Ritual was intended to pacify God and make Him favorable to the worshipper, and so in their minds the entire system tended only to emphasize the gulf that separated Man from God.

What the nexus of cause and effect was by which

this system operated to produce the result of reconciling God to the worshipper was a question which they never attempted to face; for had they, after the example of their patriarch, determinedly wrestled with the problem of why their Law was what it was, that Law would have shone forth with a self-illuminating light which would have made clear to them that all the teaching of Moses and the Prophets and the Psalms was concerning that grand ideal of a Divine Humanity which it was the mission of Jesus to proclaim and exemplify.

But they would not face the question of the *reason* of these things. They had received a certain traditional interpretation of their Scriptures and their Ritual and, as Jesus said, made the real commands of God void by their traditions. They were tied by "authorities," and this at second hand. They did not inquire what Moses meant, but only followed on the lines of what somebody else said he meant; in other words, they would not think for themselves. They were content to say, "Our Law and Ritual are what they are because God has so ordered them"; but they would not go further and inquire why God ordered them so.

With them, the whole question of revelation became the question whether *Moses* had or had not made such an announcement of the Divine will, and so their religion rested ultimately only on historical evidences. But they did not face the question, "How am I to know that the so-called prophet ever received any communication from the Divine at all?" In the last resort, there can be only one criterion by which to judge the truth of any claim to a Divine communication, which is that the message should present an intelligible sequence of cause and effect.

No man can prove that God has spoken to him; the only possible proof is the inherent truth of the message, making it appeal to our feelings and our reason with a power that carries conviction with it. The Spirit of Truth shall convince you, said the Master; and when this inner conviction of Truth is felt, it will invariably be found that, by thinking it out carefully, the reason of the feeling will manifest itself in an intelligible sequence of cause and effect. Short of realizing such a sequence, we have not realized the Truth. The only other proof is that of practical results, and to this test the Master tells us to bring the teaching that we hear; and the teaching He bid us judge by this standard was His own.

It is a principle that no great system can endure for ages, exercising a widespread and permanent influence over large masses of mankind, without *any* element of Truth in it. There have been, and still are, great systems influencing mankind which contain many and serious errors, but what has given them their power is the Truth that is in them and not the error; and careful inquiry into the secret of their vitality will enable us to detect and remove the error.

Now had the leaders of the Jews investigated their national system with intelligence and moral courage, they would have argued that its manifest vitality and elevating spiritual tone showed that it contained a great and living Truth. This Truth could not be in the mere external observances prescribed by its Law, for no nexus of cause and effect was traceable between the external observances and the promised results, and therefore the vitalizing Truth must be in some principle which supplied the connection that was apparently wanting. They would have argued that God could not have arbitrarily commanded a set of meaningless observances, and that therefore these observances must be the expression of some LAW inherent in the very nature of Man's being.

In a word, they would have realized that, to be true at all, a thing must be within the all-embracing Law of cause and effect, and that religion itself could be no exception to the rule—it must, in short, be *natural* because, if God be ONE, He cannot introduce anywhere an arbitrary and meaningless caprice subversive of the principle of Order throughout the universe. To suppose the introduction of anything by a mere act of Divine Volition, without a foundation in the sequence of the Universal Order, would be to deny the Unity of God, and thus to deny the Divine Being altogether.

Had the rulers of Israel, therefore, understood the meaning of the first two Commandments, they would have realized that their first duty, as instructors of the people, was to probe the whole Mosaic system until they reached the bedrock of cause-and-effect on which it rested. But this is just what they did not do. Their reverence for names was greater than their reverence for Truth, and, assuming that Moses taught what he never did, they put to death the Teacher of whom Moses had prophesied as the One who should complete his word in building up "the People of the I AM."

Thus they rejected "the Stone of Israel," and in so doing they fought against God—that is, against the Law of Spirit in Self-evolution. For it was this Law, and this only, that the Carpenter of Nazareth taught. He came not to destroy the teachings of Moses and of the Prophets, but to fulfill by showing what it was that, under various veils and coverings, had been handed down through the generations. It was His mission to complete the Building of the Temple by exhibiting Perfected Man as the apex of the Pyramid of Evolution.

Broad and strong and deep was laid the foundation of this Pyramid in that first movement of the ONE which the Bible tells of in its opening words; and thenceforward the building has progressed through countless ages till Man, now sufficiently developed intellectually, requires only the final step of recognizing that the Universal Spirit reaches, in him, the reproduction of itself in individuality to take his proper place as the crown and completion of the whole evolutionary process. He has to realize that the opening statement of Scripture concerning himself is not a mere figure of speech but a practical fact, and that he really is the image and likeness of the Universal Spirit.

This was the teaching of Jesus. When the Jews sought to stone Him for saying that God was His Father (John 10:31), He replied by quoting the 82d Psalm, "I said ye are gods," and laid stress on this as "Scripture that cannot be broken"—that is, as written in the very nature of things, that *signatura rerum** by which each thing has its proper place in the universal order. He replied in effect, "I am only saying of Myself what your own Law says of every one of you. I do not set Myself forth as an exception, but as the example of what the nature of every man truly is." The same mistake has been perpetu-

*"Signature of things"—*Ed.*

ated to the present day; but gradually people are beginning to see what the great truth is which Jesus taught and which Moses and the Prophets and the Psalms had proclaimed before Him.

Perfected Man is the apex of the Evolutionary Pyramid, and this by a necessary sequence. First comes the Mineral Kingdom, lying inert and motionless, without any sort of individual recognition. Then comes the Vegetable Kingdom, capable of assimilating its food, with individual life, but with only the most rudimentary intelligence, and rooted to one spot. Next comes the Animal Kingdom, where intelligence is manifestly on the increase, and the individual is no longer rooted to a single spot physically, yet is so intellectually, for its round of ideas is limited only to the supply of its bodily wants.

Then comes the fourth or Human Kingdom, where the individual is not rooted to one spot either physically or intellectually, for his thought can penetrate all space. But even he has not yet reached Liberty, for he is still the slave of "circumstances over which he has no control": his thoughts are unlimited, but they remain mere dreams until he can attain the power of giving them realization. Unlimited power of conception is his, but to complete his evolution he must acquire a corresponding power of creation. With that he will arrive at Perfect Liberty.

Throughout the Four Kingdoms which have yet been developed, the progress from the lower to the higher is always towards greater liberty, and therefore, in accordance with that principle of Continuity which Science recognizes as nowhere broken in Nature, Perfect Liberty must be the goal towards which the evolutionary process is tending.

One state more is necessary to complete the Pyramid of Manifested Nature: the addition of a Fifth Kingdom, which shall complete the work for which the four lower Kingdoms are the preparation—the Kingdom in which Spirit shall be the ruling factor, and thus the Kingdom of Spirit which is the Kingdom of God.

These considerations bring out into a very clear light one meaning of Daniel's prophecy of "the Stone," cut out without hands, which grew until it filled the whole earth.* It is the same "Stone" of which Jesus spoke and is bound by the inevitable sequence of Evolution to become the Chief Corner-Stone—that is, the angular or five-pointed stone in which all four sides of the Pyramid find their completion. It is that headstone capping the whole, of

*Daniel 2:34,35—*Ed.*

which it is written that it shall be brought forth with shoutings of "Grace, grace unto it" (Zech. 4:7).

The Fifth Kingdom, the Kingdom of spiritually developed Man, is that which is now slowly growing, as one individual after another awakes to the recognition of his own spiritual nature, seeing in it not a mere vague religious sentiment but an actual working principle to be consciously used in everything that concerns himself. This "Kingdom of God," or of Spirit, was compared by the Master to leaven hidden in meal, which spread by a silent process until the whole was leavened.

The establishment of this Fifth Kingdom is a natural process of growth, a great silent revolution which will gradually change the face of society by first changing its spirit; and for this reason the Master said, "The Kingdom of God cometh not with observation." Outward forms of government will perhaps always vary in different countries, but the recognition of Man as the true Temple must produce the same effects of "justice, mercy, and truth" in every land, so that war and crime, ignorance and want, sickness and fear shall be known no more, and sorrow and sighing shall flee away (Isaiah 35:10).

This is the meaning of the Building of the Temple, and in studying it we must remember that the sacred symbols apply not only to Man but also to his environment. The Tabernacle of Moses and the Temple of Solomon not only represent the Microcosm but also the Macrocosm. And this leads us to the threshold of a very deep mystery: the effect of the spiritual condition of the human race upon Nature as a whole, regarding which St. Paul tells us that the entire creation is waiting in anxious expectation for the revealing of the sons of God (Rom. 8:19).

The Building of the Temple is thus a threefold process, commencing with the individual man, spreading from the individual to the race, and from the race to the whole environment in which we live. This is the return to Eden, where there is nothing hurtful or destructive.

The expulsion from the spiritual "Garden of the Lord" led man into a world that brought forth thorns and thistles, and the earth was "cursed for his sake"; that is to say, the mental attitude resulting from "the Fall" induced a corresponding condition in Nature; and by the same Law, the mental attitude which is restoration from "the Fall" will produce a corresponding renovation of the material world, a state of things which is described with poetic imagery in the eleventh chapter of Isaiah.

This influence of the human race upon their surroundings, whether for good or for evil, is only the natural result of carrying out to its final consequences the initial proposition of the Bible that Man is the image of God. This is the affirmation of the inherently creative power of his Thought; and if this be true, then the collective Thought of the race must be the subtle power which determines the prevailing conditions of the natural world.

The uncertain mixed conditions among which we live very accurately represent our uncertain and mixed modes of Thought. We think from the standpoint of a mixture of good and evil and have no certainty as to which is really the controlling power. Good, we say, works "within certain limits"; but who or what fixes those limits we cannot guess. In short, if we analyze the average belief of mankind as represented in Christian countries at the present day, it resolves itself into belief in a sort of rough-and-tumble between God and the Devil, in which sometimes one is uppermost and sometimes the other; and so we entirely lose the conception of a definite control by the Power of Good steadily acting in accordance with its own character and not subject to the dictation of some Evil Power which prescribes "certain limits" for it.

This balance between good and evil is undoubtedly the present state of things, but it is the reflection of our own Thought, and the remedy for it is therefore that knowledge of the inner Law which shows us that we ourselves are producing the evils we deplore. It is for this reason that the Apostle warns us against emulations, wrath, and strife (Gal. 5:20). They all proceed from a denial of the Creative Power of our Thought—in other words, the denial that Man is the "image of God." They proceed from the hypothesis that good can exist only "within certain limits," and that therefore our work must not be directed towards the producing of more good, but to scrambling for a larger share of the limited quantity of good that has been doled out to the world by a bankrupt Deity.

Whether this scramble be between individuals in the commercial world, or between classes in social life, or between nations in the glorious name of murder with the best modern appliances, the underlying principle is always that of competition based on the idea that the gain of one can only accrue by another's loss; and therefore what prevents us today from "entering into rest"* is the same cause that produced the same effect in the time of the Psalmist: "they could not enter in because of unbelief" and "they *limited* the Holy ONE of Israel."

So long as we persist in the belief that the truly

*Ps. 95:11; Heb. 4:3—*Ed.*

originating causes of things are to be found anywhere but in our own mental attitude, we condemn ourselves to interminable toil and strife.

But if, instead of looking at *conditions*, we endeavored to realize First Cause as that which acts independently of all conditions, because the conditions flow from it and not vice versa, we should see that the whole teaching of the Bible is to lead us to understand that, because Man is the image of God, he can never divest his Thought of its inherent creative power; and for this reason it sets before us the limitless goodness of the Heavenly Father as the model which in our own use of this power we are to follow. "He maketh His sun to rise on the evil and on the good, and sendeth His rain on the just and on the unjust." In other words, the Universal First Cause is not concerned with pre-existing conditions but continually radiates forth its creative energy, transmuting the evil into the good and the good into something still better; and since it is the prerogative of Man to use the same creative power from the standpoint of the individual, he must use it in the same manner if he would produce effects of Life and not of Death.

He cannot divest his Thought of its creative power, but it rests with him to choose between Life and Death according to the way in which he employs it. As each one realizes that conditions are created from within and not from without, he begins to see the force of the Master's invitation: "Come unto Me all ye that labor and are heavy laden, and I will give you rest." He sees that the only thing that has prevented him from entering into rest has been unbelief in the limitless goodness of God and in his own limitless power of drawing from that inexhaustible storehouse; and when we thus realize the true nature of the Divine Law of Supply, we see that it depends not on taking from others without giving a fair equivalent, but rather on giving good measure pressed down and shaken together.*

The Creative Law is that the quality of the Thought which starts any particular chain of cause and effect continues through every link of the chain, and therefore if the originating Thought be that of the absolute goodness-in-itself of the intended creation, irrespective of all circumstances, then this quality will be inherent not only in the thing immediately created, but also in the whole incalculable series of results flowing from it.

Therefore, to make our work *good for its own*

*Biblical expression of abundance, originally referring to grain—*Ed.*

sake is the surest way to make it return to us in a rich harvest, which it will do by a natural Law of Growth if we only allow it time to grow. By degrees, one after another finds this out for himself, and the eventual recognition of these truths by the mass of mankind must make "the desert rejoice and blossom as the rose" (Isaiah 35:1). Let each one therefore take part joyfully in the Building of the Temple, in which shall be offered, forever, the two-fold worship of Glory to God and Goodwill to Man.

CHAPTER 7

THE SACRED NAME

A POINT THAT can hardly fail to strike the Bible student is the frequency with which we are directed to the *Name* of the Lord, as the source of strength and protection, instead of to God Himself; and the steady uniformity of this practice, both in the Old and New Testaments, clearly indicates the intention to put us upon some special line of inquiry with regard to the Sacred Name. Not only is this suggested by the frequency of the expression, but the Bible gives a very remarkable instance which shows that the Sacred Name must be considered as a formula containing a summary of all wisdom.

The Master tells us that the Queen of the South came to hear the wisdom of Solomon, and if we turn to 1 Kings 10:1, we find that the fame of Solomon's wisdom, which induced the Queen of Sheba to come to prove him with hard questions, was "concerning the *Name* of the Lord." This accords with the immemorial tradition of the Jews, that the knowledge of the secret Name of God enables him who possesses it to perform the most stupendous miracles.

This Hidden Name—the "Schem-hammaphoraseh"—was revealed, they say, to Moses and taught by him to Aaron and handed on by him to his successors. It was the secret enshrined in the Holy of Holies and was scrupulously guarded by the successive High Priests. It is the supreme secret, and its knowledge is the supreme object of attainment. Thus tradition and Scripture alike point to "The NAME" as the source of Light and Life, and Deliverance from all evil.

May we not therefore suppose that this must be the veiled statement of some great Truth? The purpose of a name is to call up, by a single word, the complete idea of the thing named, with all those qualities and relations that make it what it is, instead of having to describe all this in detail every time we want to suggest the conception of it. The correct name of a thing thus conveys the idea of its whole nature, and accordingly the correct Name of God should, in some manner, be a concise statement of the Divine Nature as the Source of all Life, Wisdom, Power, and Goodness, and the Origin of all manifested being.

For this reason the Bible puts before us "the

Name of the Lord" not only as the object of supreme veneration, but also as the grand subject of study, by means of which we may command the Power that will provide us with all good and protect us from all ill. Let us, then, see what we can learn regarding this marvelous Name.

The Bible calls the Divine Being by a variety of Names, but when we have once got the general clue to the Sacred Name, we shall find that each of them implies all the others, since each suggests some particular aspect of THAT which is the All-embracing UNIT, the everlasting ONE, which cannot be divided, and any one aspect of which must therefore convey to the instructed mind the suggestion of all the others. We will therefore seek first this general clue which will throw light on more particular appellations.

I think most people will agree that the specially personal Name by which the Divine Being is called in the Bible is Jehovah. If any Name, throughout the entire range of Scriptures, seems to invest the Divine Being with a distinct individuality, it is this one; and yet when we come to inquire into its meaning, we find that it is precisely the most emphatic statement of a universality which is the very antithesis of all that we understand by the word "individual."

The clue to this discovery is contained in the

statement that God revealed Himself to Moses by the Name Jehovah (Ex. 6:3); for since the Bible contains no statement of any other revelation of the Divine Name to Moses, except that made at the burning bush, we are at once put upon the track of some connection between the Name Jehovah and the command received by Moses to tell the children of Israel that I AM had commissioned him to deliver them.

Now, the Name which in English is rendered "Jehovah" is composed of four Hebrew letters—Yod, Hé, Wau,* Hé—thus spelling "Yevé," and this is the word which we have to analyze. And this brings us to the fact that the whole Hebrew alphabet is invested with a certain symbolical character, because, in the estimation of learned Jews, it exemplifies the great principle of Evolution; for they rightly consider that Evolution is nothing else than the working of the Divine Spirit through all worlds, whether visible or invisible.

It would require a long study to take the reader through the detailed examination of every letter, but the general idea may be stated as follows: The letter Yod† is a minute mark of a definite shape, though little more than a point, and a careful

*Usually given as Vau—*Ed.*
†י—*Ed.*

inspection of the Hebrew alphabet shows that all the other letters are combinations of this initial form. It is thus the "generating point" from which all the other letters proceed, each letter being in some way or other a reproduction of the Yod; and accordingly, it has not inaptly been regarded as a symbol of the All-originating First Principle.

If, therefore, a Name was to be devised which should represent the mystery of the Divine Being as at once the Unity which includes all Multiplicity, and the Multiplicity which is included in the Unity, the logical sequence of ideas required that the Hebrew form of such a word should commence with the letter Yod. The name of the letter is suggested by the sound of the indrawing of the breath and thus indicates self-containedness. The opposite conception is that of the sending forth of the breath, which is represented by the sound Hé,* and this letter thus indicates that which is not self-contained, but which emanates from the Source of Life. Yod thus represents Essential Life, while Hé represents Derived Life.

The letter "Wau" or "Vau,"† taken alone, signifies "and" and thus conveys the idea of a "Link." This is followed by a repetition of the "Hé," so that

*ה—*Ed.*
†ו—*Ed.*

the second portion of the Sacred Name conveys the idea of a plurality of derived lives connected together by some common link and is, therefore, the symbol of the Unity passing into manifestation as the Multiplicity of all individual beings.

The whole Name thus constitutes a most perfect statement of the Divine Being as that Universal Life, which, to use the apostolic words, is "over all, and through all, and in all";* so that once more we are brought back to what the Master said was the fundamental statement of all Truth, namely, that God is THE ONE, thus indicating that Unity of Spirit from which all individualities proceed and in which they are included.

But the second portion of the Divine Name is EVE (the Hebrew Hé corresponds with the English E), which we have found to be the *individualized* Life-Principle or the Soul, and thus this portion of the Sacred Name not only denotes Multiplicity, but also indicates the fact that the derived life stands towards the Originating Life in the relation of the feminine to the masculine. If this *feminine* nature of the Soul relatively to the Universal Spirit be steadily kept in mind, it will be found to contain the key not only to many passages of Scripture, but also to many facts of Nature both in the inner and

*Ephesians 4:6—*Ed.*

outer worlds. The words of Isaiah 54:5, "Thy Maker is thine husband," are not a mere figure of speech, but a statement of the great fundamental law of human personality; and this relative femininity of the Soul, which in this passage is pronounced so unequivocally, will be found, on investigation, to be assumed as a general principle throughout Scripture.

We have already seen from the story of "the Fall" that Eve represents the soul as distinguished from the body; and just as the Bible opens with this assertion of the feminine nature of the Soul, so it closes with it, and a large portion of the magnificent symbolism of Revelation is occupied in depicting, under the form of two mystical "Women," the generalized history of the adulterous soul and of the faithful soul, which, as "the Bride," joins with "the Spirit" in the universal invitation to all who will, to drink of the water of Life and live forever.

It is, then, this mystery of the femininity of the soul as a general principle of Nature, and its necessary relation to the corresponding Masculine principle, that is the great truth enshrined in the Sacred Name Jehovah. The first letter of the name implies "self-containedness," the statement in the universal of all that we mean individually when we speak of ourselves as "I"; and the remaining portion is the form of a verb expressing continuous Being; and the whole Name therefore is the exact statement of "I AM" which was made to Moses at the burning bush.

The Name "Jehovah" is thus the concealed statement of the great doctrine of Evolution seen in its spiritual aspect. It is the statement that every form of manifestation is an unfolding of the ONE original principle, and that beside this original ONE reappearing under infinite variety of forms there *is* no other.

But further, this Name is a statement that the passing of the Unity into that infinite galaxy of Life which, though now sometimes sorrowing, is destined to become one glorious rose of myriad petals, each of which is a rejoicing creative being, can take place only through Duality. Is this a mystery? Yes, the greatest of mysteries, including all others, for it is that universal mystery of Attraction upon which all research, even in physical science, eventually abuts; and yet, that Duality must be established before Unity can pass into all the powers and beauties of external manifestation is a proposition so self-evident as to be almost absurd in its simplicity; indeed, the very simplicity of the great universal truths is a stumbling-block to many who, like Naaman,* expect something sensational.

*See 2 Kings 5.—*Ed.*

Now this very simple proposition is, that in order to do any kind of work there must not only be something that works, but also something that is worked upon; in other words, there must be both an active and a passive factor. The scope of this book will not allow me to discuss the process by which the Duality is evolved from the Unity, though physical science supplies us with very clear analogies. But in general terms, the Universal Passive is evolved by the Universal Active as its necessary complement and provides all those conditions which are required to enable the Active Principle to manifest itself in the varied forms that constitute the successive stages of Evolution; and the interaction of these two reciprocal principles throughout Nature is as clearly indicated by the Sacred Name as the principle of Unity itself.

And the Threefold nature of all defined being at once follows from the recognition of these two interacting principles, for whatever is produced by their interaction can be neither a simple reproduction of the Active principle alone nor of the Passive alone, but must be an intermingling of the two, combining in itself the nature of both, and thus possessing an independent nature of its own, which is not exactly that of either of the originating principles.

Other and very important deductions again follow from this one, but they cannot be adequately entered upon in an introductory book like the present; still, enough has now been said to show that the Name "Jehovah" contains in itself the statement of the Three Fundamental Principles of the Universe—the Unity, the Duality, and the Trinity—and by their inclusion in a single word affirms that no contradiction exists between them, but that they are all necessary phases of the Universal Truth, which is only ONE.

Much search has been made by many for what the Cabalists call "the Lost Word," that "Word of Power" the possession of which makes all things possible to him who discovers it. Great students in bygone days devoted their lives to this search, such as Reuchlin* in Germany and Pico della Mirandola† in Italy, and, so far as the outside world judges, without any result; while later centuries discredited their studies by comparison with the practical nature of the Baconian philosophy, not wotting‡ that Bacon himself was a leader in the school to which these men belonged.

*Johann Reuchlin (1455–1522), German humanist and Cabalist—*Ed.*

†Giovanni Pico della Mirandola (1463–1494), Italian humanist—*Ed.*

‡Knowing—*Ed.*

But now the tide is beginning to turn, and improved methods of scientific research are approaching, from the physical side, that One Great Centre in which all lines of truth eventually converge; and so the fast-spreading recognition of Man's spiritual nature is leading once more to the search for "the Word of Power." And rightly did the old Hebrew builders and their followers in the fifteenth, sixteenth, and seventeenth centuries connect this "Lost Word" with the Sacred Name; but whether because they purposely surrounded it with mystery, or because the simplicity of the truth proved a stumbling block to them, their open writings only indicate a search through endless mazes, while the clue to the labyrinth lay in the Word itself.

Are we any nearer its discovery now? The answer is at once Yes and No. The "Lost Word" was as close to those old thinkers as it is to us, but to those whose eyes and ears are sealed by prejudice, it will always remain as far off as though it belonged to another planet. The Bible, however, is most explicit upon this subject; and as in the children's game the hidden thimble is concealed from the seekers by its very conspicuousness, so the concealment of the "Lost Word" lies in its absolute simplicity.

Nothing so commonplace could possibly be it,

and yet the Scripture plainly tells us that its intimate familiarity is the token by which we shall know it. We need not say, "Who shall go up for us to heaven and bring it unto us, that we may hear it and do it? Neither is it beyond the sea that thou shouldest say, Who shall go over the sea for us and bring it unto us, that we may hear it and do it? But the Word is very nigh unto thee, in thy mouth and in thy heart, that thou mayest do it" (Deut. 30:12–14). Realize that the only "Word of Power" is the Divine Name, and the mystery at once flashes into light.

The "Lost Word" which we have been seeking to discover with pain, and cost, and infinite study has been all the time in our heart and in our mouth. It is nothing else than that familiar expression which we use so many times a day: I AM. This is the Divine Name revealed to Moses at the burning bush, and it is the Word that is enshrined in the Name Jehovah; and if we believe that the Bible means what it says when it tells us that Man is the image and likeness of God, then we shall see that the same statement of Being, which in the universal applies to God, must in the individual and particular apply to Man also.

This "Word" is always in our hearts, for the consciousness of our own individuality consists only in the recognition that I AM, and the assertion of our own being, as one of the necessities of ordinary speech is upon our lips continually. Thus the "Word of Power" is close at hand to everyone, and it continues to be the "Lost Word" only because of our ignorance of all that is enfolded in it.

A comparison of the teaching of Moses and Jesus will show that they are two complementary statements of the one fundamental truth of the "I AM." Moses views this truth from the standpoint of *universal* being and sees Man evolving from the Infinite Mind and subject to it as the Great Lawgiver. Jesus views it from the standpoint of the *individual* and sees Man comprehending the Infinite by limitless expansion of his own mind, and thus returning to the Universal Mind as a son coming back to his natural place in the house of his father.

Each is necessary to the correct understanding of the other, and thus Jesus came not to abrogate the work of Moses, but to complete it. The "I AM" is ever in the forefront of His teaching: "I AM the Way, the Truth, and the Life"; "I AM the Resurrection and the Life"; "Except ye believe I AM ye shall perish in your sins." These and similar sayings shine forth with marvellous radiance when once we see that He was not speaking of Himself personally, but of the Individualized Principle of Being in the generic sense which is applicable to all mankind.

What is wanted is our recognition of that innermost self which is pure spirit, and therefore not subject to any conditions whatever. All conditions arise from one combination or another of the two original conditions, Time and Space; and since these two primary conditions can have no place in essential being and are only created by its Thought, the true recognition of the "I AM" is a recognition of the Self, which sees it as eternally subsisting in its own Being, sending forth all forms at its will and withdrawing them again at its pleasure.

To know this is to know Life-in-itself; and any knowledge short of this is only to know the appearance of Life, to recognize merely the activity of the vehicles through which it functions, while failing to recognize the motive power itself. It is recognizing only "EVE" without "YOD." The "Word of Power" which sets us free is the *whole* Divine Name, and not one part of it without the other. It is the separation of its two portions, the Masculine and the Feminine, that has caused the long and weary pilgrimage of mankind through the ages.

This separation of the two elements of the Divine Name is not true in the Heart of Being, but Man, by reasoning only from the testimony of the outward senses, forcibly puts asunder what God forever joins together; and it is because the Bridegroom has thus been taken away that the children of the bridechamber have been starved upon meagre fare, coarse and hardly earned, when they ought to have feasted with continual joy.

But the Great Marriage of Heaven and Earth at last takes place, and all Nature joins in the song of exultation, a glorious epithalamium,* whose cadences roll on through the ages, ever spreading into fresh harmonies as new themes evolve from that first grand wedding march which celebrates the eternal union of the Mystical Marriage.

When this union is realized by the individual as subsisting in himself, then the I AM becomes to him personally all that the Master said it would. He realizes that it is in him a deathless principle and that though its mode of self-expression may alter, its essential Beingness, which is the I Myself consciousness in each of us, never can; and so this principle is found to be in us both Life and Resurrection. As Life, it never ceases, and as Resurrection, it is continually providing higher and higher forms for its expression of itself, which is *ourself*.

No matter what may be our particular theory of the specific *modus operandi*† by which this renewal takes place, there can be no mistake about the principle; our physical theory of the Resurrection may be wrong, but the Law that Life will always provide a suitable form for its self-expression is

*A song or poem in celebration of a bridal couple—*Ed.*
†"Method of procedure"—*Ed.*

unchangeable and universal, and must, therefore, be as true of the Life-Principle manifesting itself as the individuality which I AM, as in all its other modes of manifestation.

When we thus realize the true nature of the I AM that I AM—that is, the Beingness that I Myself AM—we discover that the *whole* principle of Being is in ourselves—not "Eve" only, but "YOD" also; and this being the case, we no longer have to go with our pitcher to draw temporary draughts from a well outside, for now we discover that the exhaustless spring of Living Water is within ourselves.

Now we can see why it is that except we believe in the I AM, we must perish in our sins, for "sin is the transgression of the Law," and ignorant infraction of the Law will bring its penalty as certainly as wilful infraction. "Ignorantia legis neminem excusat"* is a legal maxim which obtains throughout Nature, and the innocent child who ignorantly applies a light to a barrel of gunpowder will be as ruthlessly blown up as the anarchist who perishes in the perpetration of some hideous outrage. If, therefore, we ignorantly controvert the Law of our own Being, we must suffer the inevitable consequences by our failure to rise into that Life of Liberty and Joy which the full knowledge of the power of our I AMness must necessarily carry with it.

*"Ignorance of the law excuses no one"—*Ed.*

Let us remember that Perfect Liberty is our goal. The perfect Law is the Law of Liberty. The Tree of Life is the Tree of Liberty, and it is not a plant of spontaneous growth; but as the centre of the Mystical Garden, it is its chief glory and therefore deserves the most assiduous cultivation. But it yields its produce as it grows and does not keep us waiting till it reaches maturity before giving us any reward for work; for if maturity means a point at which it will grow no more, then it will never reach maturity, for since the ground in which this Tree has its root is the Eternal Life-in-itself, there is nowhere in the universe any power to limit its growth, and so, under intelligent cultivation, it will go on expanding into increasing strength, beauty, and fruitfulness forever.

This is the meaning of the Scriptural saying, "His reward is with him and his work before him."* Ordinarily, we should suppose it would be the other way; but when we see that the possibilities of self-expansion are endless and depend on our intelligent study and work, and that at every step of the way we are bound to derive all present benefit from the degree of knowledge we are working up to, it becomes clear that the sacred text has kept the right order, and that always our reward is *with* us and our work *before* us; for the reward is the

*Isaiah 40:10 and 62:11 — *Ed.*

continually increasing joy and glory of perpetually unfolding Life.

All along the line our progress depends on working up to the knowledge we possess, for what we do not act up to we do not really believe; and the power which will overcome all difficulties is confidence in the Eternal Life-in-ourself, which is the individualized expression of the ONE I AM that spoke to Moses at the burning bush.

For what is meant by the burning bush? Surely, as we see the refugee feeding Jethro's flock in the solitudes of the desert and gazing on the Fire enveloping the bush without consuming it, we realize that here again we are turning over the pages of a sacred picture-book, which first attracts the little child with its vivid scenes painted in glowing colors of a wonderful Eastern life in the dim far-back ages, which prompts him as he grows older to ask the meaning of the pictures, and which at last reveals it to him in the discovery that they are pictures neither of the East nor of the West, not of this century nor of that, but of all time and of all place, and that he himself is the central figure in them all.

The Bible is the picture-book of the evolution of Man, and this particular picture of the "burning bush" is that of human individuality in its unity with the all-enveloping Fire of the Universal Spirit of Life. The "bush" represents "Wood," which, under its Greek name of *"hulé,"* we recognize as the generic term for "Matter"; and the "burning bush" thus signifies the union of Spirit and Matter into a single whole, that perfectness of manifested Being in which the lower principles of the individual are recognized as forming the vehicle for the concentration of the All-originating Spirit. The "bush" still remains a bush, but it is a glorified bush sending forth a glorious aura of warmth and light, from the midst of which proceeds the creative voice of the I AM.

This is the great truth symbolized by the revelation to Moses as he fed his father-in-law's flock in the wilderness, and, as the same revelation comes to each of us now, the words of that other Prophet of whom Moses spoke become clear to us, and we see that by realizing the true being of the I AM in ourselves, we grasp that principle which will put an end to our infraction of the Law, because it is the very Law itself forever becoming personal with our own personality.

This, then, is the great truth which we learn from the Name "Jehovah." As the Name is infinite, so also will be the expansions of its meaning; but this book not being infinite, I have been able only to touch on the broad outlines of its vastness; still, enough has been said to give the clue we were seeking, to elucidate the meaning of other forms of the Sacred Name.

Naturally, the reader will first think of that other

Name, of which it is written that there is none other under heaven whereby we may be saved, which statement at once confronts us with the astonishing assertion that we are saved by a *Name*. "What's in a name?" asks Shakespeare—or Bacon (?)* A good deal, we may suppose, when we meet with such a statement as this, or its Old Testament equivalent, "the Name of the Lord is a strong tower; the righteous runneth into it and is safe."

But we have already found that the Great Name of the Old Testament is something very different from a merely personal appellation, and the same is true of the Great Name of the New Testament also. It is, indeed, the Name of that Prophet of the I AM whom Moses predicted as completing the work which he had begun; but precisely because He is *the* Representative Man of all ages, His Name must represent all that constitutes Perfected Humanity.

And it is so with a Divine simplicity. It is the combination of the earthly name with the heavenly: Jesus, at the time a very common name among the Jews, and Christ, which is not a name but a description, "the Anointed One." Each name is the proper complement of the other, and together they indicate the sublime truth that the anointing of the

*An allusion to the "Shakespeare-Bacon controversy": was William Shakespeare a pseudonym for Francis Bacon?—*Ed.*

Divine Spirit is the birthright of every human being, only awaiting our recognition of our true nature to show itself with power. The carpenter—the workman with his everyday name—is the Christ; and the lesson to be learned is that the ONE I AM is in every man, and that that forming of Christ in us which St. Paul speaks of is a personal development in accordance with recognizable laws inherent in every human being. If Christ is the Great Example, it must be as the Example of that which we have it in us to become, and not of something entirely foreign to our nature; and it is because of this community of nature that He is "the first-born among many brethren."*

The space at my disposal will not allow me to enter here into the deeply important questions of the Nativity and the Resurrection. The Bible affirms them both, and they are the necessary and logical results of that specialized and selective line of Evolution of which I have spoken on page 6; but to show the sequence of cause and effect by which this is brought about, and its dependence upon the initial *Impersonal* nature of the Universal Mind, is not to be done in a few pages.

If, however, I should meet with sufficient encouragement from the readers of the present volume, I hope to follow it up with another in

*Romans 8:29—*Ed.*

which these topics will be discussed, and in the meanwhile we may learn from the generalization contained in the Great Name of the New Testament that lesson of the Brotherhood of Humanity which the Master has impressed upon us in the words "The King shall answer and say unto them, Verily I say unto you, inasmuch as ye have done it unto one of the least of these My brethren, ye have done it unto Me" (Matt. 25:40). The Name of Jesus Christ is, therefore, the proclamation of the inherent Divine nature of Man, with all its limitless possibilities, and is thus once more the statement of the Bible's initial proposition that Man is made in the image and likeness of God.

And these thoughts recall yet another of the Divine Names which teaches the same lesson: Immanuel, "God with us," or, as it might perhaps be better rendered, "God in us," "Immanent God," the finding of God *in ourselves*, which is in exact accordance with the Master's teaching that the Kingdom of Heaven is *within* us. This Name, which occurs in Isaiah 7:14, speaks for itself, and should be compared with the description given in Isaiah 9:6,7, which is the old familiar Christmas text, "Unto us a child is born," etc. Now, whoever the "us" may be, the prophet clearly speaks of the Wonderful Child as being born to them. They are the parents and He is their Child. But in the description which follows, we are told equally clearly that He is "the Everlasting Father"; and the teaching of Jesus leaves us in no doubt that "the Father" is the Divine All-creating Spirit, which is therefore "the Father" of the "us" who are the parents of the Child.

This lands us in a curious paradox. There can be no reasonable doubt that the word "us" is here spoken of human personalities, and that in the same breath the Divine Being who is spoken of as their Father is announced to them as their Child. We have therefore here a sequence of three generations: the Father of the parents, the "us" who are the parents, and the Child who is born to them; and since the Father of the parents and the Child of the parents is said to be the same Being, there is no avoiding the conclusion that the Wonderful Child is his own Grandfather, and vice versa.

This is one of those sacred puzzles of which many instances occur in the Bible, and whose meaning is clear enough when we know the answer, and the purpose of which is to lead us to look for an answer, which will put us in possession of the great truth which it is the purpose of all Scripture to teach us. The riddle propounded by Isaiah, "What is that which becomes its own grandson?" is substantially the same with which the Master posed the scribes when He asked them how David's son could at the same time be his Lord (Luke 20:41); and the identity of the question is apparent from the fact that in the passage in Isaiah we are told that this Wonderful Child shall sit on the throne of David.

A further description of him occurs in Isaiah 11:1, where we again find the same three stages—first Jesse, next the stem proceeding out of Jesse, and lastly the Rod or Branch growing out of the stem. Now Jesse is the father of David, and therefore "the Branch" is the same person regarding whom Isaiah and Jesus propounded their conundrums. Placing these four remarkable passages together, we get the following description of the Wonderful Child:

> His name is Immanuel.
> His father's name is David.
> His grandfather's name is Jesse.
> And He is His own grandfather and Lord over His father.

What is it that answers to this description? Again we find the solution of the enigma in the names. "Jesse" means "to be," or "he that is," which at once brings us back to all we have learned concerning the Universal I AM—the ONE Eternal Spirit which is "the Everlasting Father."

"David" means "the Beloved," or the man who realizes his true relation to the Infinite Spirit; and the description of Daniel as a man greatly beloved and who had set his heart to understand (Daniel 10:11) shows us that it is this set purpose of seeking to understand the nature of the Universal Spirit and the mode of our own relation to it that raises the individual to the position of David or "the Beloved."

This is in strict agreement with the Master's teaching to the woman of Samaria,* that the Eternal Spirit, which is "the Father," *seeks* those who will worship, not according to this or that traditionary form, but in spirit and in truth, having a real knowledge of what it is they worship and of the true nature of the mental act they perform. "We *know* what we worship" is the mark by which Jesus distinguishes the worship of the "Israelites indeed," the "People of the I AM," from that of the Samaritans, though fully recognizing the right intention of their worship of the "unknown God."†

It was after his successful wrestling with the Divine Being, and in consequence of his determination not to let go until it had been fully revealed, that Jacob obtained the name of "Israel."

*John 4—*Ed.*
†A play on Acts 17:23 in the context of John 4:22—*Ed.*

Then from the individual's illuminated recognition of the Truth of Being—the discovery that he himself is the concentration of the Universal Spirit into particular personality—there necessarily arises the reproduction of the Universal Spirit in the Individual Mind. This is *re*-generation; that is to say, the second generating of the Divine UNIT as another Unity or manifestation of itself in the form of the Individual, in no way differing in nature from the original All-embracing Unit, but only in the mode of expression, having now become individual personality with all the attributes of personality.

On the plane of the universal, the place of these more highly specialized attributes was held by a *generic* tendency towards life-givingness, increase, and beauty; and this generic tendency the reproduced Unit now follows up with the additional powers it has evolved by the attainment of self-recognizing individuality.

The new personality thus generated may be considered as the child of the individual soul which gives birth to it; and since there is only ONE Spirit anywhere and everywhere, it can be only another mode of the original ONE. Consequently, the "Son" who is thus born to David "the Beloved" is Himself "the Everlasting Father," and thus the answer to the sacred puzzle is that the man who has really learned the inner meaning of the words "know thyself" discovers that the true I AM in himself is one with the Universal I AM, which is the root of all individualized being.

It is in the light of these sublime truths that the Name of "the Son" is equally with that of "the Father" the Sacred Name, in the true knowledge of which salvation is alone to be found. For what do we mean by "Salvation"? "That we might be saved from the hand of all that hate us,"* is the answer; that is, from the power of everything that in any way militates against our enjoyment of the fullest life. That we might attain to continually increasing degrees of Life was the declared object of the Master's mission, and, therefore salvation means the power to ask and receive that our joy may be full; and the only way this power can ever come to us is by the recognition of our own possibilities as being each of us the image and likeness of God.

Therefore it is written, "to them gave He power to become the Sons of God, even to them that believe in His Name"; and the word rendered "power" may also be rendered as "right," so that this passage assures us both of our power and right to take possession of our inheritance as sons and daughters of the Almighty. Now mark well that this

*Luke 1:71—*Ed.*

promise is not held forth as a reward for the acceptance of some theological speculation, which conveys no real meaning to us, and which by its very terms must be incapable of proof; but it is the natural and logical outcome of the initial proposition with which the Bible opens, that Spirit is the ONE and Only Source, Origin, and Substance of all things, a self-evident truth the contrary of which it is impossible to conceive.

What I here call "Spirit" you may, if you please, call "the Unknowable," or *x*, or denote it by a single stroke; the name or symbol we choose is quite immaterial, so long as we grasp the fact that the initial Originating Power must of necessity reproduce itself all the way down the scale, no matter how different the forms under which it does so. In whatever way we may denote it, it is always the Great Expressor; and all that is, we ourselves included, is its Expression of itself; so that the whole teaching of Truth may be summed up in the words "The Expressor and the Expressed are ONE."

Work out the problem in any way you will and you will never arrive at any other final result than this; and so we always come back to that fundamental axiom which Jesus announced as the supreme statement of the LAW. This is the great truth enshrined in every form of the Sacred Name; and therefore it is that every form of the Great

Name, when rightly understood, is found to be "the Word of Power."

But we must never forget that the opening description of Man, as made in the image and likeness of God, has added to it the words "male and female created He them"; and if we grasp the full significance of this statement, we shall see that the recognition of Truth is not complete unless we realize the place of the Passive or Feminine element in Being. It is for this reason that in ancient times initiation could be entered upon either along the Doric or Ionic line,* the former being more especially the initiation for males and the latter for females; but by whichever line it was commenced, a perfect initiation implied a return along the opposite line, in accordance with St. Paul's dictum that "neither is the man without the woman, neither the woman without the man, in the Lord" (1 Cor. 11:2), and therefore there are not wanting in Scripture statements of the Sacred Name answering to this fact.

One of the most remarkable of these is found in Hosea 2:16: "And it shall be at that day, saith the Lord, that thou shalt call Me Ishi, and shalt call Me no more Baali." What is the meaning of this change of Name? Realize that a name has a *meaning*, and it becomes clear that some radical

*That is, in the Greek "Mysteries" tradition—*Ed.*

change must be intended. But this cannot be any change in the Divine Being, for from first to last the Scripture bears emphatic testimony to the unchangeableness of "God." "I am the Lord, I change not; therefore ye sons of Jacob are not consumed," says the Old Testament (Malachi 3:6). "The Father of lights with whom there is no variableness, neither shadow of turning," says the New (James 1:17).

The change cannot, then, be in the nature of "God," and therefore cannot be a change in the Law by which that nature expresses itself; consequently, it can only be a change in the *conditions* under which that Law is working. Now this is precisely the sort of change that is spoken of. "Baali" means Lord, the master of a servant, the proprietor of a slave. "Ishi," on the other hand, means "Husband," and the change of name therefore indicates a change in the condition of some feminine element towards its correlative masculine element.

This corresponding change is stated in Isaiah 62:4: "Thou shalt no more be termed Forsaken, neither shall thy land any more be termed Desolate; but thou shalt be called Hephzibah, and thy land Beulah; for the Lord delighteth in thee, and thy land shall be married." The word "Hephzibah" is rendered in the margin "my delight," which is sufficiently significant, but its derivation is from the

Semitic root "*hafz,*" which in all its combinations always carries the idea of protection or guarding; and the name Hephzibah may therefore be more accurately rendered "a guarded one," thus at once recalling the words in which the New Testament describes those "who by the power of God are *guarded* through faith unto salvation" (1 Peter 1:5, R. V.)

Now the change indicated by these names is that of a female slave who is set free by her master and then married by him, and I think it would be impossible to hit upon a more accurate analogy for describing the emancipation of the soul from bondage and its establishment in a relation of confidence and love towards the Divine Universal Mind.

We must never forget the feminine nature of the soul relatively to the Universal Mind. Their union produces the Wonderful Child who shall rule all things, and who is the Essential Male called in the Bible "the Son"; but the soul itself is, and always must be, feminine. Until she becomes illuminated, the soul can only conceive of God as a master whom she is bound to obey, and hence she strives to keep in His good graces by sacrifices, ceremonies, and observances of all sorts—He is "Baali" and must be propitiated. But when the liberating light breaks upon her, she discovers that the Universal Principle has hitherto held this relation to her because she had conceived of it only in this way and had thus provided it only with such conditions as compelled it to exhibit itself in this form.

Now she learns that these conditions are not imposed by the Universal Principle itself, but that it must of necessity follow that line of expression which each particular individuality opens up for it; and when this is clearly perceived, with all the consequences that flow from it, the soul finds that she is no longer a slave but is in perfect Liberty, and that her relation to the Great Mind is that of a beloved wife, guarded, honored, and treated on terms of equality.

This is the truth illustrated, as St. Paul tells us, in the allegory of Sarah and Hagar. Hagar, the slave, is expelled, and Sarah, the Princess, takes her place. These two symbolical women, like the two "women" of Revelation, indicate two opposite conditions of the soul; and similarly their "sons," like the offspring of those two other "women," represent the respective powers which these two conditions of soul generate—the one living in the wilderness of secondary causes and becoming an archer—that is, relying upon the use of external means, not understanding the true nature of causation, and therefore dependent for his results upon just happening to make a good shot, and often making very bad ones—the other, like Isaac, the acknowledged heir of all the Father's possessions, assuming gradually more and more of his powers and responsibilities until, by the combined influence of natural growth and careful training, he at last attains that mature development which qualifies him to participate in the administration of the paternal authority.

The true relation of the individual soul to the Universal Principle could not be more perfectly depicted than by the names Ishi and Hephzibah. We have only to turn to any well-ordered family to see the force of the illustration. The respective spheres of the husband and wife as the heads of such a household are clearly defined. The husband provides the supplies and the wife distributes them, and each has that confidence in the other which renders any interference with one another's action quite unnecessary.

This is the precise analogue of the relation between the individual and the Universal Mind. The individual mind is not the creator of power, but the distributor of it, just as in physical science we realize that we do not create energy, but only change its form and direction. But exactly as the universal store of Nature from which we draw physical energy does not dictate to us in what form, in what quantities, or for what purpose we shall use it, so in like manner the Universal Principle does not dictate the specific conditions under which it is to be employed, but will manifest itself according to any conditions that we may provide for it by our own mental attitude; and therefore the only limitations to be laid upon our use of it are those arising from the Law of Love. Liberty without Love is Destruction, and Love without Liberty is Despair.

Just as in photography we need for the production of a perfect image the combined action of an accelerator and a restrainer,* so to produce perfect images of the Divine strength, beauty, and gladness, we require a self-projecting force which is the full liberty of Creative Power, combined with a directing and restraining force which is the tenderness of wisdom and love; and so in the description of the Perfect Woman we read that in her mouth is the Law of Kindness. Hephzibah, the Perfect Woman, rules her household wisely in love and so applies the raw material, which she can draw from her husband's storehouse without stint, that, by her diligence and understanding, she converts it into all those varied forms of use and beauty which are indicated under the similitudes of domestic provision and merchandise in the thirty-first chapter of Proverbs.

*I.e. of the chemical reactions—*Ed.*

We find, then, two aspects of the Sacred Name: one which presents it as the Universal I AM, the All-productive Power which is the root of all manifestation, and thus includes all individualities within itself, involving them in the circulus of its own movement; and the other indicative of the reciprocal relation between this Power and the individual soul. But there is yet a third aspect under which this Power may be viewed, and that is as *working through the individual* who has become conscious of his own relation to it and of his consequent direction and instruction by it. In this sense the Old Testament enumerates its Names in the text I have already quoted: "His Name shall be called Wonderful, Counsellor, the Mighty God, the Everlasting Father, and the Prince of Peace" (Isaiah 9:6). In the Book of Job this is called "the Interpreter" (3:23), and in the New Testament this Name is called "The Word."

What may be the nature of the Divine Self-consciousness in itself is a matter on which we can in no way profitably speculate; to do so is trying to analyze that which, as the starting-point of all else, must necessarily be incapable of analysis for the simple reason that there can be nothing before the First. But what we *can* realize is the mode in which we experience our own relation to the Originating Spirit, and this will be found to form a threefold recognition of it, corresponding with what I have said above. Our primary recognition of the Spirit is that of an All-embracing Universal Principle, a simple Unity; but gradually we shall come to find that our perception of this Unity contains enfolded in it a threefold relation to our personality which implies the existence of a corresponding threefold aspect in the Unity.

We must always recollect that all we can know of God is our own consciousness of our relation to Him, and eventually we shall find that this relation is, first, generic, as to the Creating Spirit; secondly, specific, as forming a particular *class* of individuals holding a special relation to the Spirit; and thirdly, individual, as differentiated units of this particular class. Thus by a Law of Reciprocity, we realize "the Father" or Parent Spirit, "the Son" or Divine Ideal of Human Personality, and "the Holy Spirit" as the operation of the Original Spirit upon the individual, resulting from the individual's recognition of his relation to the Father in a Divine Sonship. Seen in this light, the doctrine of the Trinity in Unity ceases to be either a contradiction in terms or the conception of a limiting anthropomorphism, but on the contrary it is found to be the statement of the highest experiences of the human soul.

With these preliminary remarks, I would lay particular stress upon the Name given to the Universal

Principle in its Third aspect, that of manifestation through the individual mind. In this sense it is emphatically called "The Word," and a study of comparative religions shows that this conception of the Universal Mind, manifesting itself as Speech, has been reached by all the great race-religions in their deeper significances. The "Logos" of Greek philosophy, the "Vach" of the Sanskrit, are typical instances, and the reason is to be found, as in all statements of truth, in the nature of the thing itself.

The Biblical account of creation represents the work as completed by the appearing of Man; that is to say, the evolutionary process culminates in the Creative Principle expressing itself in a form differing from all lower ones in its capacity for reasoning. Now reasoning implies the use of words either spoken or employed mentally, for whether we wish to make the stages of an argument plain to another or to ourselves, it can only be done by putting the sequence of cause and effect into *words*.

The first idea suggested by the principle of Speech is, therefore, that of individual intelligence, and next, as following from this, we get the idea of expressing individual will; then, as we begin to realize the reciprocal relation between the Universal Mind and the individual mind, which necessarily results from the latter being an evolution from the former, our conception of intelligence and volition becomes extended from the individual to the Universal, and we see that because these qualities exist in human personality, they must exist *in some more generalized mode* in that Universal Mind, of which the individual mind is a more specialized reproduction; and so we arrive at the result that the Speech-principle is the highest expression of the Divine Wisdom, Power, and Love, whose combined action produces what we call Creation.

In this sense, then, the Bible attributes the creation of the world to the Divine Word, and it therefore rightly says that "In the beginning was The Word, and The Word was with God, and The Word was God," and that without The Word "was not anything made that was made"; and from this commencement, the natural sequence of evolution brings us to the crowning result in the manifestation of The Word as Man, at first ignorant of his Divine origin, but nevertheless containing all the potentialities which the recognition of his true nature as the image of God will enable him to develop. And when at length this recognition comes to anyone, he arises and returns to "The Father," and in the discovery of his true relation to the Divine Mind finds that he also is a child of the Almighty and can speak "the Word of Power."

He may have been the prodigal who has wasted his substance, or the respectable brother who thought that only limited supplies were doled out to him; but as soon as the truth dawns upon him, he realizes the meaning of the words "Son, thou art ever with Me, and all that I have is thine." In its Third aspect as "the Word," the Universal Principle becomes specialized. In its earlier modes it is the Life-Principle working by a Law of Averages, and thus maintaining the race as a whole, but not providing special accommodation for the individual. And it is inconceivable that the Cosmic Power, *as such*, should ever pass beyond what we may call the administration of the world *in globo*,* for to suppose it doing so would involve the self-contradiction of the Universal acting on the plane of the Particular without becoming the particular; and it is precisely by *becoming* the particular, or by evolution into individual minds, that it carries on the work beyond the stage at which things are governed by a mere Law of Averages.

It is thus that we become "fellow-workers with God" and that "the Father" is represented as inviting His sons to work in His vineyard. By recognition of his own true place in the scheme of evolution, Man learns that his function is to *carry on* the work which has been begun in the Universal to still further applications in the Particular, thus affording

*I.e. in a global sense—*Ed.*

the key to the Master's words, "My Father worketh *hitherto, and* I work"; and the instrument by which the instructed man does this is his knowledge of the Sacred Name in its Threefold significance.

The study of the Sacred Name is the study of the Livingness of Being and of the Law of Expression in all its phases, and no book or library of books is sufficient to cope with such a vast idea. All any writer can do is to point out the broad lines of the subject, and each reader must make his own personal application of it. But the Law remains forever that the sincere desire for Truth produces a corresponding unfoldment of Truth, and the supreme Truth is reached in that final recognition of the Divine Name, "God is Love."

CHAPTER 8

The Devil

It is impossible to read the Bible and ignore the important part which it assigns to the Devil. The Devil first appears as the Serpent in the story of "the Fall" and figures throughout Scripture till the final scene in Revelation, where "the old Serpent, which is the Devil and Satan," is cast into the lake of fire. What, then, is meant by the Devil? We may start with the self-obvious proposition that "God" and the "Devil" must be the exact opposites of each other. Whatever God is, the Devil is not. Then, since God alone *is*, the Devil *is not*. Since God is Being, the Devil is Not-Being. And so we are met by the paradox that though the Bible says so much about the Devil, yet the Devil does not exist. It is precisely this fact of nonexistence that makes up the Devil; it is that power which in appearance is, and in reality is not; in a word, it is the Power of the Negative.

We are put upon this track by the statement in

2 Corinthians 1:20 that in Christ, all the promises of God are Yea and Amen—that is, *essentially Affirmative*; in other words, that all our growth towards Perfected Humanity must be by recognition of the Positive and not by recognition of the Negative. The prime fact of Negation is its Nothingness; but owing to the impossibility of ever divesting our Thought of its Creative Power, our *conception* of the Negative as something having a substantive existence of its own becomes a very real power indeed, and it is this power that the Bible calls "the Devil and Satan," the same old serpent which we find beguiling Eve in the Book of Genesis. It is equally a mistake to say that there is an Evil Power or that there is not. Let us examine this paradox.

A little consideration will show us that it is impossible for there to be an Infinite and Universal Power of Evil, for unless the Infinite and Universal Power were *Creative*, nothing could exist. If it be creative, then it is the Life-Principle working always for self-expression, and to suppose the undifferentiated principle of Life acting otherwise than life-givingly would contradict the very idea of its livingness.

Whatever tends to expand and improve life is the Good, and therefore it is a primary intuition from which we cannot get away that the Infinite,

Originating, and Maintaining Power can only be Good. But to find this absolute and unchangeable "Good," we require to get to the very bedrock of Being, to that as yet undifferentiated Life-in-itself inherent in, and forming one with, Universal primordial Substance, of which I have spoken in a former chapter. This All-underlying Life is forever expressing itself through Form; but the Form is not the Life, and it is from not seeing this that so much confusion arises.

The Universal Life-Principle, simply as such, finds expression as much in one form as another, and is just as active in the scattered particles which once made a human body as it was in those particles when they cohered together in the living man; this is merely the well-recognized scientific truth of the Conservation of Energy.

On the other hand, we cannot help perceiving that there is something in the individual which exercises a greater power than the perpetual energy residing in the ultimate atoms; for otherwise what is it that maintains in our bodies for perhaps a century the unstable equilibrium of atomic forces which, when that something is withdrawn, cannot continue for twenty-four hours? Is this something another something than that which is at work as the perpetual energy within the atoms? No, for otherwise there would be two originating powers in the

Universe, and if our study of the Bible teaches us anything, it is that the Originating Power is only ONE; and we must therefore conceive of the Power we are examining as the same Power that resides in the ultimate atoms, only now working at a higher level. It has welded the atoms into a distinct organism, however lowly, and so to distinguish this mode of power from the mere atomic energies, we may call it the Integrating Power, or the Power which Builds up.

Now evolution is a continuous process of building up, and what makes the world of today a different world from that of the ichthyosaurus and the pterodactyl is the successive building up of more and more complex organisms, culminating at last in the production of Man as an organism both physically and mentally capable of expressing the Life of the Supreme Intelligence by means of Individual Consciousness. Why, then, should not the Power, which is able to carry on the race as a perpetually improving expression of itself, do the same thing *in the individual*? That is the question with which we have to deal; in other words, why need the individual die? Why should he not go on in a perpetual expansion?

This question may seem absurd in the light of past experience. Those who believe only in blind forces answer that death is the law of Nature, and those who believe in the Divine Wisdom answer that it is the appointment of God. But strange as it may seem, both these answers are wrong. That death should be the ultimate law of Nature contradicts the principle of continuity as exemplified in the Lifeward tendency of evolution; and that it is the will of God is most emphatically denied by the Bible, for that tells us that he that has the power of death is the Devil (Hebrews 2:14). There is no beating about the bush; not God but the Devil sends death. There is no getting out of the plain words. Let us examine this statement.

We have seen that whatever God is, the Devil must be the opposite, and therefore if God is the Power that builds up, the Integrating Power, the Devil must be the power that pulls down, or the Disintegrating Power. Now what is Disintegration? It is the breaking up of what was previously an "integer" or perfect Whole, the separation of its component parts. But what is it that causes the separation? It is still the Building-up Power, only the Law of Affinity by which it works is now acting from other centres, so as to build up other organisms.

The Universal Power is still at its building work, only it seems to have lost sight of its original motive in the organism which is falling to pieces and to have taken up fresh motives in other directions. And this is precisely the state of the case; it is just the want of continuous motive that causes disintegration. The only possible motive of the All-originating Life-Principle must be the expression of *Life*, and therefore we may almost picture it as continually seeking to embody itself in intelligences which shall be able to grasp its motive and cooperate with it by keeping that motive constantly in mind.

Granted that this *individualization of motive* could take place, there appears no reason why it should not continue to work on indefinitely. A tree is an organized centre of life, but without the intelligence which would enable it to individualize the *motive* of the Universal Life-Principle. It individualizes a certain measure of the Universal Vital Energy, but it does not individualize the Universal Intelligence, and therefore when the measure of energy which it has individualized is exhausted, it dies; and the same thing happens with animals and men.

But as the particular intelligence advances in the recognition of itself as the individualization of the Universal Intelligence, it becomes more and more capable of seizing upon the *initial motive* of the Universal Mind and giving it permanence. And supposing this recognition to be complete, the logical result would be never-ceasing and perpetually expanding individual life, thus bringing us back to those promises which I have quoted in the opening pages of this book, and reminding us of the Master's statement to the woman of Samaria that "the Father" is always "seeking" those who will worship Him in spirit and in truth; that is, those who can enter into the spirit of what "the Father" is aiming at.

But what happens in the absence of a perfect recognition of the Universal Motive is that sooner or later the machinery runs down, and the "motive" is transferred to other centres where the same process is repeated, and so Life and Death alternate with each other in a ceaseless round. The disintegrating process is the Universal Builder taking the materials for fresh constructions from a tenement without a tenant; that is, from an organism which has not reached the measure of intelligence necessary to perpetuate the Universal Motive in itself, or, as the Master put it in the parable of the ten virgins, such as have not a supply of oil to keep their lamps burning.

This Negative disintegrating force is the Integrating Power working, so to say, at a lower level relatively to that at which it had been working in the organism that is being dissolved. It is not another power. Both the Bible and common sense tell us that ultimately there can be only ONE power in the Universe, which must, therefore, be the

Building-power, so that there can be no such thing as a power which is negative *in itself*; but it shows itself negatively *in relation to the particular individual*, if through want of recognition he fails to provide the requisite conditions for it to work positively.

Work it always will, for its very being is ceaseless activity; but whether it will act positively or negatively towards any particular individual depends entirely on whether he provides positive or negative conditions for its manifestation, just as we may produce a positive or negative current according to the electrical conditions which we supply.

We see, then, that what gives the Positive Power a negative action is the failure to intelligently recognize our own individualization of it. In the lower forms of life this failure is inevitable, because they are not provided with an organism capable of such a recognition. In Man the suitable organism is present, but he seeks knowledge only from past experiences, which have necessarily been of the negative order, and does not, by the combined action of reason and faith, look into the Infinite for the unfoldment of limitless possibilities; and so he employs his intelligence to deny that which, if he affirmed it, would be in him the spring of perpetual renovation.

The Power of the Negative, therefore, has its

root in our denial of the Affirmative; and so we die because we have not yet learned to understand the Principle of Life; we have yet to learn the great Law, that "the higher mode of intelligence controls the lower." In consequence of our ignorance, we attribute an affirmative power to the Negative—that is to say, the power of taking an initiative on its own account, not seeing that it is a *condition* resulting from the absence of something more positive; and so the power of the Negative consists in affirming that to be true which is not true, and for this reason it is called in Scripture the father of lies, or that principle from which all false statements are generated.

The word "Devil" means "false accuser" or "false affirmer," and this name is therefore in itself sufficient to show us that what is meant is the creative principle of Affirmation used in the wrong direction, a truth which has been handed down to us from old times in the saying "Diabolus est Deus inversus."* This is how it is that "the Devil" can be a vast impersonal power while at the same time having no existence, and so the paradox with which we started is solved. And now also it becomes clear why we are told that "the Devil" has the power of death. It is not held by a personal individual, but

*Literally, "The Devil is God inverted"—*Ed.*

results quite naturally from that ignorant and inverted Thought which is "the Spirit that denies."

This is the exact opposite to "the Son of God," in whom all things are only "Yea and Amen." That is the Spirit of the Affirmative and, therefore, the Spirit of Life; and so it is that the Son of God was manifested that "He might destroy him that had the power of death, that is, the Devil, and deliver them who, through fear of death, were all their lifetime subject to bondage" (Hebrews 2:14,15).

Again, we are told that the Devil is Satan. This name appears to be another form of "Saturn" and may also be connected with the root "sat" or "seven," Saturn being in the old symbolical astronomy the outermost or seventh planet. In that system the centre is occupied by Sol or the Sun, which represents the Life-giving Principle, and Saturn represents the opposite extreme, or Matter at the point furthest removed from Pure Spirit.

Now, taken in due order, Matter or Concrete Form is as necessary as Spirit itself, for without it there could be no manifestation of Spirit; in other words, there could be no *ex*istence at all. Seen from this point of view, there is nothing evil in it, but on the contrary, it may be compared to the lamp which concentrates the light and gives it a particular direction, and in this aspect Matter is called

"Lucifer" or the Light-bearer. This is Matter taking its proper place in the order of the Kingdom of Heaven. But if "Lucifer" falls from heaven, becomes rebellious, and endeavors to usurp the place of "Sol," then it is the fallen Archangel and becomes "Satan," or that outermost planet which moves in an orbit whose remoteness from the warmth and light of the Sun renders all human life and joy impossible, a symbolism which we retain in our common speech when we say that a man has a saturnine aspect.

Thus "Satan" is the same old serpent that deceived Eve; it is the wrong belief that sets merely secondary causes, which are only *conditions*, in the place of First Cause or that originating power of Thought which makes enlightened Man the image of his Maker and the Son of God.*

But we must not make the mistake of supposing that because there is no Universal Devil in the same sense as there is Universal God, therefore there are no individual devils. The Bible frequently speaks of them, and one of the commissions given by the Master to His followers was to cast out devils.

*For the all-important distinction between Causes and Conditions, see Chapter 9 of my *Edinburgh Lectures on Mental Science*.

The words used for *the* Devil are, in the Greek, "Diabolos," and, in the Hebrew, "Satan," both having the same general meaning of the Principle of Negation; but individual devils are called in the Hebrew, "sair," a hairy one, and, in the Greek, "daimon," a spirit or shade, and these terms indicate evil spirits having personal identity.

Now without stopping to discuss the question whether there are orders of spiritual individualities which have never been human, let us confine our attention to the immense multitudes of disembodied human spirits which, under any hypothesis, must crowd the realms of the unseen. Can we suppose them all to be good? Certainly not, for we have no reason to suppose that mere severance from its physical instrument either changes the moral quality or expands the intelligence of the mind, and therefore if there is such a thing as survival after death at all, we cannot conceive of the other world otherwise than as containing millions upon millions of spirits in various stages of ignorance and ill-will, and consequently ready to make the most unscrupulous use of their powers where opportunity offers.

The time is fast passing away when it will be possible to regard such a conception as fantastic, and taking our stand simply upon the well-ascertained ground of thought-transference and telepathy, we may well ask, if such powers as these can be exercised by the spiritual entity while still clothed in flesh, why should they not be equally, or even more powerfully, employed by spirits out of the flesh?

This opens an immense field of inquiry which we cannot stop to investigate; but setting aside all other classes of evidence on this subject, the experimentally ascertained facts of telepathy bring to light possibilities which would explain all that the Bible says regarding the malefic influence of evil spirits. But the inference to be drawn from this is not that we should go in continual terror of obsession or other injury, but that we should realize that our position as "sons and daughters of the Almighty" places us beyond the reach of such malignant entities.

Our familiar principle, the Law of Attraction, is at work here also. Like attracts like; and if we would keep these undesirable entities at a distance, we can do so most effectually by centering our thoughts on those things which we *know* from their nature cannot invite evil influences. Let us follow the apostolic advice, and "whatsoever things are true, whatsoever things are honest, whatsoever things are just, whatsoever things are pure, whatsoever things are lovely, whatsoever things are of good report; if there be any virtue and if there be any praise, think on these things" (Philippians 4:8).

Then, however far the Law of Attraction may

extend from us into the other world, we may rest assured that it will only act to bring us in touch with that innumerable company of angels and spirits of just men made perfect, of whom we are told in the twelfth chapter of Hebrews, and who, because they are joined in the same worship of the ONE Divine Spirit as ourselves, can only act in accordance with the principles of harmony and love.

I will not attempt the analysis of so important a subject in the short space at my disposal, but I would caution all students against tampering with anything that savors of ceremonial magic. However little acknowledged in public, it is by no means infrequently practised at the present day, and, if on no other grounds, it should be resolutely shunned as a powerful system of autosuggestion capable of producing the most disastrous effects on those who employ it. No New Thought reader can be ignorant of the power of autosuggestion, and I would therefore ask each one to think out for himself what the tendency of autosuggestion conducted on such lines as these must be. "I speak as unto wise men, judge ye what I say."*

The Bible is by no means silent on this subject, but I may sum up its teaching in a few lines. It assumes, throughout, the possibility of intercourse†

*1 Corinthians 10:15—*Ed.*

†I.e. exchange of thoughts or feelings—*Ed.*

between men and spirits, but, with the exception of the Master's temptation, where I understand a symbolic representation of the general principle of evil—the Power of the Negative which we have already considered—it should be remarked that all its record is of appearances of good angels as ministering spirits to heirs of salvation.

Nor were these visitants sought after by those who received them; their appearance was always spontaneous; and the solitary instance which the Bible records of a spirit appearing whom it was sought to raise by incantation is of the appearance of Samuel to Saul, announcing that his rebellion had culminated in this act of witchcraft, and this was followed by the suicide of Saul on the next day.

If, then, our study of the Bible has led us to the conclusion that it is the statement of the Law of the inevitable sequences of cause and effect, this uniform direction of its teachings must indicate the presence of certain sequences in this connection also, which follow definite laws, although we may not yet understand them. This knowledge will come to us by degrees with the natural expansion of our powers, and when it arrives in its proper order, we shall be qualified to use it; and if we realize that there is a Universal Mind capable of guiding us at all, we may trust it not to keep back from us anything it is necessary we should know at each stage of our onward journey. Do we want knowledge? The Master has promised that the Spirit of Truth shall guide us into all truth. "Should not a people seek unto their God instead of unto them that have familiar spirits?" (Isaiah 8:19). There is a *reason* at the back of all these things.

We thus see that the whole question of the power of evil turns on the two fundamental Laws which I spoke of in the opening pages of this book as forming the basis of Bible teaching: the Law of Suggestion and the Law of the Creative Power of Thought. The conception of an abstract principle of evil, the Devil, receives its power from our own autosuggestion of its existence; and the power of evil spirits results from a mental attitude which allows us to receive their suggestions.

Then in both cases, the suggestion having been accepted, our own creative power of Thought does the rest and so prepares the way for receiving still further suggestions of the same sort. Now the antidote to all this is a right conception of God or the Universal Spirit of Life as the ONE and only *originating* Power. If we realize that relatively to us this Power manifests itself through the medium of our own Thought, and that in so doing it in no way changes its inherent quality of Life-givingness, this recognition must constitute such a supremely powerful and all-embracing Suggestion as must necessarily eradicate all suggestions of a contrary description; and so our Thought, being based on this Supreme Suggestion of Good, is certain to have a correspondingly life-giving character.

To recognize the essential One-ness of this Power is to recognize it as God, and to recognize its essential Life-givingness is to recognize it as Love, and so we shall realize in ourselves the truth that "God is Love." Then "if God be for us, who can be against us?" and so we realize the further truth that "perfect love casteth out fear," with the result that in our own world there can be no devil.

CHAPTER 9

The Law of Liberty

Nothing is more indicative of our ignorance regarding the purpose and meaning of the Bible than the distinction which it is often sought to draw between the Law and the Gospel. We are told of different "dispensations," as though the Divine method of conducting the world changed after the fashion of political constitutions. If this were the case, we should never know under what system of administration we were living, for we could only be informed of these alterations by persons who were "in the know" with the Divine Power, and we should have nothing but their bare assertion to depend on, that they were "in the know."

This is the logical outcome of any system which is based upon the allegation of specific determinations by a Divine Autocrat. It cannot be otherwise, and therefore all such systems are destined sooner or later to fall to pieces, because their foundation of so-called "authority" crumbles away under the scrutiny of intelligent investigation. The Divine orderings can only be known by the Divine workings, and the intelligent study of the Divine working is the only criterion which the Bible, rightly understood, anywhere sets up for the recognition of Truth.

The whole of the Psalms are based entirely on this principle, and the Master claimed their testimony to His mission. He himself spoke of tradition as rendering void the true Law of God; and so far from claiming to introduce any new dispensation, he emphatically declared that his special business was to fulfil the Law—that is, to demonstrate it in all its completeness. If the Law taught by Moses is true, and the Gospel preached by Jesus is true, then they are both true together and are simply statements of the same Truth from different standpoints; and the proofs of their truth will be found in their agreement with one another and with the universal principles of Natural Law which we can learn by the study of ourselves and of our environment.

If the Old and New Testaments are right in saying that the foundation of all other knowledge is that God is ONE, then we may be certain that we are on a wrong track if we think that Divine truth can be different at one time to what it is at another. We realize the principle of "continuity" throughout physical nature, and if we see that the physical must originate in the spiritual, we cannot deny the extension of "continuity" throughout the entire system; and therefore, if the messages of the Old and New Testaments are both true, we may expect to find the same principle of "continuity" running through both. On investigation this will be found to be the case, and no truer definition can be given of the Gospel than that it is the Law worked out to its logical conclusions.

The Law which the Bible sets forth from first to last is the Law of Human Individuality. The Bible is the spiritual Natural History Book of Man. It begins with his creation by evolution from the kingdoms which had preceded him, and it terminates with his apotheosis. The line is long, but it is straight and reaches its glorious destination by an orderly sequence of cause and effect. It is the statement of the evolution of the individual as the result of his recognition of the Law by which he came to be a human being at all.

When he sees that this happened neither by chance nor by arbitrary command, then, and not till then, will he wake up to the fact that he is what he is by reason of a Law inherent in himself, the action of which he can therefore carry on indefinitely by correctly understanding and cheerfully following it.

His first general perception that there is such a Law at all is followed by the realization that it must be the Law of his own individuality, for he has only discovered the existence of the Law by recognizing himself as the Expression of it; and therefore he finds that, before all else, the Law is that he shall be *himself*. But a Law which allows us to be entirely *ourselves* is Perfect Liberty, and thus we get back to St. James' statement that the Perfect Law is the Law of Liberty.

Obviously it is not Liberty to allow ourselves to be depressed into such a mental attitude of submission to every form and degree of misery as coming to us "by the will of God" that we at last reach a condition of apathy in which one blow more or less makes very little difference. Such teaching is based on the Devil's beatitude—"Blessed are they that expect nothing, for they shall not be disappointed"—but that is not the Gospel of Deliverance which Jesus preached in His first discourse in the synagogue of Nazareth. Jesus' teaching was not the deification of suffering, but the fulness of Joy; and He emphatically declared that all bondage—everything which keeps us from enjoying our life to the full—is the working of that Power of the Negative which the Bible calls the Devil. To give up hope and regard ourselves as the sport of an inexorable fate is not Liberty. It is not obedience to a higher power, but abject submission to a lower—the power of ignorance, unintelligence, and negation.

Perfect Liberty is the consciousness that we are not thus bound by any power of evil, but that, on the contrary, we are centers in which the Creative Spirit of the Universe finds particular expression. Then we are in harmony with its continual progressive movement towards still more perfect modes of expression, and therefore its thought and our thought, its action and our action, become identical, so that in expressing the Spirit we express ourselves. When we reach this unity of consciousness, we cannot but find it to be perfect Liberty; for our own self-expression, being also that of the All-creating Spirit as it manifests in our individuality, is no longer bound by antecedent conditions, but starts fresh from the standpoint of Original Creative Energy.

This is Liberty, according to Law, the law of the All-creating Harmony, in which God's way and our way coincide. The idea of Liberty, without a unifying Harmony as its basis, is inconceivable, for with everyone *struggling* to get their own way *at somebody else's expense*, you create a pandemonium; and that is just why there is so much of that element in the world at the present time. But such an inverted idea of liberty is based on the assumption that Man does not possess the power of controlling his conditions by his Thought; in other words, the flat denial of the initial statement of Scripture regarding him that he is made "in the image and likeness of God."

Once grant the creative power of our Thought and there is an end of *struggling* for our own way, and an end of gaining it *at someone else's expense*; for, since by the terms of the hypothesis we can create what we like, the simplest way of getting what we want is not to snatch it from somebody else, but to make it for ourselves; and since there is no limit to Thought, there can be no need for straining; and for everyone to have his own way in *this* manner would be to banish all strife, want, sickness, and sorrow from the earth.

Now, it is precisely on this assumption of the creative power of our Thought that the whole Bible rests. If not, what is the meaning of being saved by Faith? Faith is essentially Thought; and therefore every call to have Faith in God is a call to trust in the power of our own Thought about God. "According to your faith be it unto you," says the New Testament. "As a man thinketh in his heart so is he," says the Old Testament. The entire Book is nothing but one continuous statement of the Creative Power of Thought.

The whole Bible is a commentary on the text "Man is the image and likeness of God." And it comments on this text sometimes by explaining why, by reason of the ONE-ness of the Spirit, this must necessarily be so; sometimes by incitements to emotional states calculated to call this power into activity; sometimes by precepts warning us against those emotions which would produce its inverse action; sometimes by the example of those who have successfully demonstrated this power, and conversely by examples of those who have perverted it; sometimes by statements of the terrible consequences that must inevitably follow such perversion; and sometimes by glorious promises of the illimitable possibilities residing in this wonderful power, if used in the right way; and thus it is that "all Scripture is profitable for doctrine, for reproof, for correction, for instruction in righteousness."*

All this proceeds from the initial assumption with which the Bible starts regarding Man, that he is the reproduction in individuality of that which God is in universality. Start with this assumption, and the whole Bible works out logically. Deny it, and the Book becomes nothing but a mass of inconsistencies and contradictions. The value of the Bible as a storehouse of knowledge and a guide into

*2 Timothy 3:16—*Ed.*

Life depends entirely on our attitude with regard to its fundamental proposition.

But this proposition contains in itself the Affirmation of our Liberty; and the Gospel preached by Jesus amounts simply to this, that if anyone realizes himself as the reproduction, in conscious individuality, of the same principles which the Law of the Old Testament bids us recognize in the Divine Mind, he will thereby enter upon an unlimited inheritance of Life and Liberty. But to do this we must realize the Divine image in ourselves *on all lines.*

We cannot enter upon a full life of Joy and Liberty by trying to realize the Divine image along one line only. If we seek to reproduce the Creative Power without its correlatives of Wisdom and Love, we shall do so only to our own injury; for there is one thing which is impossible alike to God and Man, and that is to plant a seed of one sort and make it yield fruit of another. We can never get beyond the Law that the effect must be of the same nature as the cause. To abrogate this Law would be to destroy the very foundation of the Creative Power of Thought, for then we could never reckon upon what our Thought might produce; so that the very same Law which places creative power at our disposal necessarily provides punishment for its misuse and reward for its right employment.

And this is equally the case along the two other lines. To seek development only on the line of Knowledge is to contemplate a store of wealth while remaining ignorant of the one fact which gives it any value: that it is *our own*; and, in like manner, to cultivate only Love makes our great motive power evaporate in a weak sentimentality which accomplishes nothing, because it does not *know how* and does not *feel able*. So here we see the force of the Master's words when he bids us aim at a perfection like that of our "Father" in heaven, a perfection based on the knowledge that all being is threefold in essence and one in expression; and that therefore we can attain Liberty only by recognizing this universal Law in ourselves also; and that, accordingly, the Thought that sets us free must be a simultaneous movement along all three lines of our nature.

The Divine Mind may be represented by a large circle and the individual mind by a small one, but that is no reason why the smaller circle should not be as perfect for its own area as the larger; and therefore the initial statement of the Bible that Man is the image of God is the charter of Individual Liberty for each one, provided we realize that this likeness must extend to the whole threefold unity that is ourself, and not to a part only.

Our Liberty, therefore, consists in being ourselves in our *Wholeness*, and this means the conscious exercise of *all* our powers, whether of our visible or invisible personality. It means being ourselves, not trying to be somebody else.

The *principles* by which anyone ever attains to self-expression, whether in the humblest or the most exalted degree, are always the same, for they are *universals* and apply to everyone alike, and therefore we may advantageously study their working in the lives of others; but to suppose that the expression of these principles is bound to take the same form in us that it did in the individual who is the object of our hero-worship, is to deny the first principle of manifested being, which is Individuality.

If someone towers above the crowd, it is because he has grown to that height, and I cannot permanently attain the same elevation by climbing on his shoulders, but only by growing to the same height myself. Therefore, the attempt to copy a particular individual, however beautiful his character, is bondage and a relinquishing of our birthright of Selfhood.

What we have to do in studying those lives which we admire is to discover the universal principles which those persons embodied in their way, and then set to work to embody them in *ours.* To do this is to realize the Universal I AM manifesting itself in every Individuality; and when we see this, we find that the statement of the Law of Individual Liberty is the declaration that was made to Moses at the burning bush and is the truth which Jesus proclaimed when He said that it was the recognition of the I AM that would set us free from the Law of bondage and death.

In speaking of the I AM as the Principle of Life, neither Jesus nor Moses used the words personally, and Jesus especially avoids any such misconstruction by saying, "If I bear witness of Myself, My witness is not true"; in other words, He came to set forth not Himself personally, but those great principles common to all mankind, of which He exemplified the full development.

When a little child is first told that God made the world, it accepts the statement without doubting, but immediately and logically follows it up with the question, then who made God? And the unsophisticated mother very often gives the correct answer, God made Himself. There is the whole secret, and when we come down—or rather when we rise—to the level of these souls whose pure intuitions have not been warped by arguments drawn only from the outside of things, we see that the principle of continual self-creation into all varieties of individuality affords the true clue to all that we are and to all that is around us; and when we see this, the teaching regarding the I AM in ourselves becomes clear, logical, and simple.

Then we understand that the Law of our *Whole* Being—that which is Cause as well as Effect—is the reproduction in Individuality of the same Power which makes the worlds; and when this is understood in its Wholeness, we see that this principle cannot, as manifested in us, be in opposition to its manifestation of itself in other forms. The Whole must be homogeneous; that which is homogeneous cannot act in opposition to itself; and consequently this homogeneous principle, which underlies all individuality and is the I AM in each, can never act contrary to the true Law of Life. Therefore, to know ourselves as the concentration of this principle into a focus of self-recognition is to be at one with the Life-Principle which is all that is in all worlds and under all forms.

It is this recognition of our own Individuality as being a reproduction of the Universal Principle in the *whole* personality that constitutes belief in "the Son," or the principle of spiritual sonship, which brings us out of the bondage of ignorance and impotence into the liberty of knowledge and power.

But the reader who is still within the trammels of the traditional exegesis will probably say, if this be so, what is meant by such texts as that contained in the fifty-third chapter of Isaiah, "He was wounded for our transgressions," etc.? and the answer is that the personality here spoken of is still the same Typical Man—the Divine Son—who is described by Isaiah as "the Wonderful Child," only seen from another point of view. This is the description of him in his prenatal stage, that is, before his manifestation as the Son whose Name is Wonderful, Counsellor, etc.

And this brings us to the consideration of a very recondite subject, the question whether "Spirit" ever does pass into unconsciousness. Whether from the physiological or the psychological side, there is important evidence tending to the conclusion that "Spirit" is never in a condition of unconsciousness; and if this is the case with that concentration of *pure* Spirit which is the individualized I AM in each of us, how can we conceive its suffering from those transgressions of the Law of our own being which result in all the misery, pain, and death that the world has witnessed?

If the Spirit in us is the very Impersonation* of the Law of Life, what woundings, what bruisings it must suffer in the course of educating the lower principles into self-recognition and spontaneous

*I.e. "assumption of the character of" minus the prevalent sense of "with fraudulent intent"—*Ed.*

compliance with the true Law of the Individuality in its Wholeness!

Then we see that it is only by the infinite persistence of the Spirit, in its struggle towards perfecting the vehicles of its Self-expresison, that the Individuality in all its completeness can ever be brought to maturity and the crown set to the work of Evolution which commenced far back in the dim unfathomable past. We realize St. Paul's meaning in saying that the Spirit groans with unutterable groanings, for it is that principle which St. John tells us cannot sin (1 John 3:9 and 5:18), that is, cannot act contrary to the true Law of Being; and thus a peculiar emphasis is set on the injunctions "Grieve not the Spirit," "Quench not the Spirit," for the individualized Spirit is the intensely Living Centre of ourselves—the I AM that I Myself AM in every one of us.

The question of the ultimate consciousness of the individuality under the outward semblance of unconsciousness, as in trance, or under the conditions induced by hypnotism, or anesthetics, involves problems of a scientific character which I hope to have an opportunity of discussing on another occasion; but even supposing there is no such latent consciousness of suffering as I have suggested, we may well transfer the whole description of the fifty-third chapter of Isaiah to the conscious sufferings of the outer man. That, at any rate, is a "man of sorrows and acquainted with grief," and the reason of these sufferings is the want of Wholeness; they are the result of trying to live only in one portion of our nature—and that the lower—instead of in the Whole, and consequently these sufferings will continue until we realize that even balance of all parts of our nature which alone constitutes true *individuality*, or that which is without division.

By the buffetting of experience, the lower personality is being continually driven to inquire more and more into the *reason* of its sufferings, and as it grows in intelligence, it sees that they always result from some wilful or ignorant infraction of the Law of Things-as-they-are, as distinguished from Things-as-they-look; and so by degrees the lower personality grows into union with the higher personality, which itself is the Law of Things-as-they-are become Personal, until at last the two are found to be ONE, and the Perfected Man stands forth Whole.

This is the process to which the writer of the Epistle to the Hebrews refers when he says that "though he were a son, yet learned he obedience by the things which he suffered," thus indicating a course of education which can only apply to a personality whose evolution is not yet completed. But by these sufferings of the lower personality the salvation of the entire individuality is at length accomplished, for, being thus led to study the Law of the

Whole, the lower or simply intellectual mentality at last discovers its relation to the Intuitive and Creative Principle and realizes that nothing short of the harmonious union of the two makes a Complete Man. Until this recognition takes place, the real meaning of suffering is not understood.

To talk about "the Mystery of Pain" is like talking of the mystery of broken glass if we throw a stone at a window—it is of our own making. We attribute our sufferings to "the will of God" simply because we can think of nothing else to attribute them to, being ignorant alike of ourselves as centres of causation and of God as the Universal Life-Principle, which cannot will evil against anyone.

So long as we are at this stage of intelligence, we esteem the lower personality (the only self we yet know) to be "stricken and smitten of God"—we put it all down to God's account—while all the time the cause of our wounding and bruising was not the will of God, but our own transgressions and iniquities; transgression: the infraction of the Law of Causation; and iniquity: unequalness, or the want of even balance between all portions of our Individuality, without which the liberating recognition of our own I AM-ness can never take place.

This reading of this wonderful chapter* takes it out of the region of merely speculative theology and

*Isaiah 53.—*Ed.*

brings it into a region where we can understand its statements as links in a chain of cause and effect connecting the promised redemption with facts that we know, and starting from causes whose working is obvious to us.

This reading in no way detracts from the value of this passage as a prophecy of the great work of the Master, for it is a generic description applicable to each, in his degree, who in any way labors or suffers for the good of others; and the description is therefore supremely applicable to Jesus, in whom that perfect Individualization of the Divine of which we speak was fully accomplished.

The Law of Man's Individuality is therefore the Law of Liberty, and equally it is the Gospel of Peace; for when we truly understand the Law of our own individuality, we see that the same Law finds its expression in everyone else, and consequently we shall reverence the Law in others exactly in proportion as we value it in ourselves. To do this is to follow the golden rule of doing to others what we would they should do unto us; and because we know that the Law of Liberty in ourselves must include the free use of our own creative power, there is no longer any inducement to infringe the rights of others, for we can satisfy all our desires by the exercise of our knowledge of the Law.

As this comes to be understood, cooperation will take the place of competition with the result of removing all ground of enmity, whether between individuals, classes, or nations; and thus the continual recognition of the Divine or "highest" principles in ourselves brings "peace on earth and good-will among men" naturally in its train, and it is for this reason that the Bible everywhere couples the reign of peace on earth with the Knowledge of God.

The whole object of the Bible is to teach us to be ourselves and yet more ourselves. It does not trouble itself with political or social questions, or even with those of religious organization, but it goes to the root of all, which is the Individual. First set people right individually, and they will naturally set themselves right collectively. It is only applying to mankind the old proverb "Take care of the pence and the pounds will take care of themselves"; and therefore the Bible deals only with the two extremes of the scale, the Universal Mind and the Individual Mind. Let the relation between these two be clearly understood, and all other relations will settle themselves on lines which, however varied in form, will always be characterized by individual Liberty working to the expression of perfect social harmony.

CHAPTER 10

The Teaching of Jesus

In this chapter I shall endeavor to give a connected idea of the general scope and purpose of the Master's teachings, the point of which we in great measure miss by taking particular sayings separately, and so losing the force which pertains to them by reason of the place they hold in His system as a whole. For, be it remembered, Jesus was teaching a definite system—not a creed, nor a ritual, nor a code of speculative ethics, but a system resulting from the threefold source of spiritual inspiration, intellectual reasoning, and experimental* observation, which are the three modes in which the Universal Mind manifests itself as Conscious Reasoning Power or "the Word." And therefore this system combines the religious, philosophical, and scientific characters, because it is

*Here in the sense of "experiential"—*Ed.*

a statement of the action of universal principles at the level where they find expression through the human mind.

As we proceed, we shall find that the basis of this system is the same perception of the unity between the Expressor and the Expressed which is also the basis of the teaching of Moses, and which is summed up in the significant phrase I AM. Jesus brings out the consequences of this Unity in their relation to the Individual and therefore presupposes the teaching of Moses, regarding the Universal Unity, as the necessary foundation for its reflection in the individual.

The great point to be noted in the teaching of Jesus is His statement of the absolute liberty of the individual. That was the subject of His first discourse in the synagogue of Nazareth (Luke 4:16); He continued His teaching with the statement, "the truth shall make you free"; and He finished it with the final declaration before Pilate that He had come into the world to the end that He should bear witness to the Truth (John 18:37). Thus, to teach us the knowledge of Liberating Truth was the beginning, the middle, and the end of the great work which the Master set before Him.

Now, there are two facts about this teaching that deserve our special attention. The first is that the perfect liberty of the individual must be in accordance with the will of God; for on any other supposition Jesus would have been teaching rebellion against the Divine will; and therefore any system of religion which inculcates blind submission to adverse circumstances as submission to the will of God must do so at the cost of branding Jesus as a leader of rebellion against the Divine authority.

The other point is that this freedom is represented simply as the result of coming *to know the Truth.* If words mean anything, this means that Liberty in truth exists at the present moment, and that what keeps us from enjoying it is simply our ignorance of the fact. In other words, the Master's teaching is that the essential and therefore ever-present Law of each individual human life is absolute Liberty; it is so in the very nature of Being, and it is only our ingrained belief to the contrary that keeps us in bondage to all sorts of limitation.

Of course, it is easy to explain away all that the Master said by interpreting it in the light of our past experiences; but these experiences themselves constitute the very bondage from which He came to deliver us, and therefore to do this is to destroy His whole work. We do not require His teaching to go back to the belittling and narrowing influence of past experiences; we do that naturally enough so long as we remain ignorant of any other possibilities. It is just this being tied up that we want to get loose from, and He came to tell us that, when we know the Truth, we shall find we are not tied up at all. If we hold fast to the initial teaching of Genesis, that the Divine Principle makes things by *itself becoming* them, then it follows that when it becomes the individual man, it cannot have any other than its own natural movement in him—that is, a continual pushing forward into fuller and fuller expression of itself, which therefore becomes fuller and fuller life in the individual; and consequently, anything that tends to limit the full expression of the individual life must be abhorrent to the Universal Mind expressing itself *in that individuality*.

Then comes the question as to the way in which this truth is to be realized; and the practical way inculcated by the Master is very simple. It is only that we are to take this truth for granted. That is all. We may be ready to exclaim that this is a large demand upon our faith; but after all, it is the only way in which we ever do anything. We take all the operations of the Life-Principle in our physical body for granted, and what is wanted is a similar confidence in the working of our spiritual faculties.

We trust our bodily powers because we assume their action as the natural Law of our being; and in just the same way we can only use our interior powers by tacitly assuming them to be as natural to us as any others. We must bear in mind that from first to last the Master's teaching was never other than a *veiled* statement of Truth: He spoke "the word" to the people in parables, and "without a parable spake He not unto them" (Matt. 13:34). It is indeed added "and when they were alone He expounded all things to His disciples"; but if we take the interpretation of the parable of the sower as a sample, we can see how very far these expositions were from being a full and detailed explanation.

The thickest and outermost veil is removed, but we are still very far from that plain speaking among "the full-grown" which St. Paul tells us was equally distant from his own writing to the Corinthians. I say this on the best authority, that of the Master Himself. We might have supposed that in that last discourse, which commences with the fourteenth chapter of St. John's Gospel, He had withdrawn the final veil from His teaching; but no, we have His own words for it that even this is a veiled statement of the Truth. He tells His disciples that the time when He shall show them plainly of "the Father" is still future (John 16:25).

He left the final interpretation to be given by the only possible interpreter, the Spirit of Truth, as the real significance of His words should in time dawn upon each of His hearers with an inner meaning that would be none other than the revelation of The Sacred Name. As this meaning dawns upon us, we find that Jesus no longer speaks to us in proverbs, but that His parables tell us plainly of "the Father," and our only wonder is that we did not discern His true meaning long ago.

He is telling us of great universal principles which are reproduced everywhere and in everything with special reference to their reproduction on the plane of Personality. He is not telling us of rules which God has laid down in one way, and could, had He chosen, have laid down in another, but of universal Laws which are the very Being of God and which are therefore inherent in the constitution of Man. Let us, then, examine some of His sayings in this light.

The thread on which the pearls of the Master's teaching are strung together is that Perfect Liberty is the natural result of knowing the Truth. "When you find what the Truth really is, you will find it to be that you are perfectly free" is the centre from which all His other statements radiate. But the final discovery cannot be made *for* you; you must each make it *for yourself*. Therefore "he that hath ears to hear let *him* hear."

This is nowhere brought out more clearly than in the parable of the Prodigal Son. The fact of sonship had never altered for either of the two brothers, but in different ways they each missed the point of their position as sons. The one limited himself by separating off a particular *share* of the Father's goods for himself, which, just because of being a limited share and not the whole, was speedily exhausted, leaving him in misery and want.

The other brother equally limited himself by supposing that he had no power to draw from his Father's stores but must wait till he in some way acquired a specific permission to do so, not realizing his inherent right, as his Father's son, to take whatever he wanted.

The one son took up a false idea of independence, thinking it consisted in separating himself and, to use an expressive vulgarism, in being entirely "on his own hook," while the other, in his recoil from this conception, went to the opposite extreme and believed himself to have no independence at all.

The younger son's return, so far from extinguishing the instinct of Liberty, gratified it to the full by placing him in a position of honor and command in his Father's house; and the elder son is rebuked with the simple words, "Why wait for me to give you what is yours already? All that I have *is* thine."

It would be impossible to state the relation between the Individual Mind and the Universal Mind more clearly than in this parable, or the two classes of error which prevent us from understanding and utilizing this relation.

The younger brother is the man who, not realizing his own spiritual nature, lives on the resources of the lower personality till their failure to meet his needs drives him to look for something which cannot thus be exhausted, and eventually he finds it in the recognition of his own spiritual being as his inalienable birthright, because he was made in the image and likeness of God and could not by any possibility have been created otherwise.

Gradually, as he becomes more and more conscious of the full effects of this recognition, he finds that "the Father" advances to meet him, until at last they are folded in each other's arms, and he realizes the true meaning of the words "I and my Father are ONE." Then he learns that Liberty is in union and not in separation, and realizing his identity with the Infinite, he finds that all its inexhaustible stores are open to him.

This is not rhapsody but simple fact, which becomes clear if we see that the only possible action of the undifferentiated Life-Principle must be to always press forward into fuller and fuller expression of itself, in particular forms of life, *in strict accordance with the conditions which each form provides for its manifestation.* And when anyone thoroughly grasps this principle of the differentiation, through form, of an entirely undistributed universal potential, then he will see that the mode of differentiation depends on the direction in which the specializing entity is reaching out.

If he further gets some insight into the boundless possibilities which must result from this, he will realize the necessity, before all things, of seeking to reproduce in individuality that Harmonious Order which is the foundation of the universal system.

And, since he cannot particularize the whole Infinite at a single stroke, which would be a mathematical impossibility, he utilizes its boundless stores by particularizing, from moment to moment, the specific desires, powers, and attractions which at that moment he requires to employ.

And, since the Energy from which he draws is infinite in quantity and unspecialized in quality, there is no limit either of extent or kind to the purposes for which he may employ it. But he can only do this by abiding in "the Father's" house, and by conforming to the rule of the house, which is the Law of Love.

This is the only restriction, if it can be called a restriction to avoid using our powers injuriously; and this restriction becomes self-obvious when we consider that the very thing which puts us in possession of this limitless power of drawing from the Infinite is the recognition of our identity with the Universal One, and that any employment of our powers to the intentional injury of others is in itself a direct denial of that "unity of the Spirit which is the bond of peace."

The binding power *(religio)* of Universal Love is thus seen to be inherent in the very nature of the Liberty which we attain by the Knowledge of the Truth; but except this, there is no other restriction. Why? Because, by the very hypothesis of the case, we are employing First Cause when we consciously use our creative power with the knowledge that our Thought is the *individual* action of the same Spirit which, in its universal action, is both the Cause and the Being of every mode of manifestation; for the great fact which distinguishes First Cause from secondary causation is its entire independence of all *conditions*, because it is not the outcome of conditions but itself creates them—it produces its own conditions step by step as it goes along.*

If, therefore, the Law of Love be taken as the foundation, *any* line of action can be worked out

*For fuller explanation regarding our use of First Cause, see my *Edinburgh Lectures on Mental Science*.

successfully and profitably; but this does not alter the fact that a higher degree of intelligence will see a much wider field of action than a lower one, and therefore if our field of activity is to grow; it can only be as the result of the growth of our intelligence; and consequently, the first use we should make of our power of drawing from the Infinite should be for steady growth in understanding.

Life is the capacity for action and enjoyment, and therefore any extension of the field for the exercise of our capacities is an increase of our own livingness and enjoyment; and so the continual companionship of the Spirit of Truth, leading us into continually expanding perception of the limitless possibilities that are open to ourselves and to the whole race, is the supreme Vivifying Influence; and thus we find that the Spirit of Truth is identical with the Spirit of Life.

It is this consciousness of companionship that is the Presence of the Father; and it is in returning to this Presence and dwelling in it that we get back to the Source of our own spiritual nature and so find ourselves in possession of boundless possibilities without any fear of misusing them, because we do not seek to be possessors of the Divine Power without being possessors of the Divine Love and Wisdom also.

And the elder brother is the man who has not

thrown off the Divine guidance as the younger had done, but who has realized it only in the light of a restriction. Always his question is "Within what limits may I act?" and consequently, starting with the idea of limitation, he finds limitation everywhere; and thus, though he does not go into a far country like his brother, he relegates himself to a position no better than that of a servant; his wages are measured by his work, his creeds, his orthodoxies, his limitations of all sorts and descriptions, which he imagines to be of Divine appointment, while all the time he has imported them himself.

But him also "the Father" meets with the gracious words, "Son, thou art *ever* with me, and all that I have *is* thine"; and therefore as soon as this elder brother becomes sufficiently enlightened to perceive that all the elements of restriction in his beliefs, save only the Law of Love, have no place in the ultimate reality of *Life*, he too reenters the house, now no longer as a servant but as a son, and joins in the festival of everlasting joy.

We find the same lesson in the parable of the Talents. The use of the powers and opportunities we have, just where we are *now*, naturally opens up sequences by which still further opportunities, and consequently higher development of our powers, become possible; and these higher developments in their turn open the way to yet further expansion, so that there is no limit to the process of growth other than what we set to it by denying or doubting the principle of growth in ourselves, which is what is meant by the servant burying his talent in the earth.

"The lord" is the Living Principle of Evolution which obtains equally on all planes, and nothing has been more fully established by science than the Law that as soon as progress stops, retrogression begins; so that it is only by continual advance we can escape the penalty with which Professor Aytoun* threatens us in his humorous verses, that we shall

> Return to the monad from which we all sprang,
> Which nobody can deny.

But on the other hand, the employment of our faculties and opportunities, so far as we realize them, is, by the same Law, certain to produce its own reward. By being faithful over a few things, we shall become rulers over many things, for God is not unmindful to forget your labor of love, and so day by day we shall enter more and more fully into the joy of our Lord.

*William Edmondstoune Aytoun (1813–65), Scottish poet and parodist—*Ed.*

The same idea is repeated in the parable of the man who contrived to get into the wedding feast without the wedding garment. The Divine Marriage is the attainment by the individual mind of conscious union with the Universal Mind or "the Spirit"; and the feast, as in the parable of the Prodigal Son, signifies the joy which results from the attainment of Perfect Liberty, which means power over all the resources of the Universe, whether within us or around us.

Now, as I have already pointed out, the only way in which this power can be used safely and profitably is through that recognition of its Source which makes it in all points subservient to the Law of Love, and this was precisely what the intruder did not realize. He is the type of the man who fails in exactly the opposite way to the servant who buries his Lord's talent in the earth. This man has cultivated his powers to the uttermost, and so is able to enter along with the other guests. He has attained that Knowledge of the Laws of the spiritual side of Nature which gives him a place at that Table of the Lord which is the storehouse of the Infinite; but he has missed the essential point of all his Knowledge, the recognition that the Law of Power is one with the Law of Love, and so, desiring to separate the Divine Power from the Divine Love, and to grasp the one while rejecting the other, he finds that the very Laws of which he has made himself master, by his knowledge, overwhelm him with their own tremendousness and by their reflex action become the servants who bind him hand and foot, and cast him into the outer darkness. The Divine Power can never be separated with impunity from the Divine Love and Guidance.

The parable of the unjust steward is based upon the Law of the subjective nature of individual life. As in all the parables, "the lord" is the supreme Self-evolving Principle of the Universe, which, relatively to us, is purely subjective, because it acts in and through ourselves. As such, it follows the invariable Law of subjective mind, which is that of response to any suggestion that is impressed upon it with sufficient power.*

Consequently, "the lord" does not dispute the correctness of the accounts rendered by the steward, but, on the contrary, commends him for his wisdom in recognizing the true principle by which to escape the results of his past maladministration of the estate.

St. Paul tells us that he is truly approved "whom the Lord commendeth," and the commendation of the steward is unequivocally stated by Jesus; and

*I have discussed this subject at greater length in my *Edinburgh Lectures on Mental Science*.

therefore we must realize that we have here the statement of some principle which harmonizes with the Life-giving tendency of the Universal Spirit. And this principle is not far to seek. It is the acceptance by "the Lord" of less than the full amount due to Him.

It is the statement of Ezekiel 18:21,22 that if the wicked man forsake his way, "he shall surely live and not die. All his transgressions that he hath committed shall not be mentioned unto him; in his righteousness that he hath done he shall live." It is what the Master speaks of as agreeing with the adversary while we are still in the way with him; in other words, it is the recognition that because the Laws of the Universe are not vindictive but simply causal, therefore the reversal of our former misemployment of First Cause, which in our case is our Thought demonstrated in a particular line of action, must necessarily result in the reversal of all those evil consequences which would otherwise have flowed from our previous wrongdoing.

I have enlarged in a previous chapter on the operation of the Law of Suggestion with regard to the question of sacrifice; and when we either see that the Law of Sacrifice culminates in No Sacrifice or reach the place where we realize that a Great and Sufficient Sacrifice has been offered up once for all, then we have that solid ground of suggestion which results in the summing-up of the whole Gospel in the simple words "Don't do it again."

If we once realize the great truth stated in Psalm 18:26 and 2 Samuel 22:27, that the Divine Universal Spirit always becomes to us exactly the correlative of our own principle of action, and that it does so naturally by the Law of Subjective Mind, then it must become clear that it can have no vindictive power in it, or, as the Bible expresses it, "Fury is not in Me" (Isaiah 27:4)

But for the very same reason, we cannot trifle with the Great Mind by trying to impress one character upon it by our thought while we are impressing another upon ourselves by our actions. This is to show our ignorance of the nature of the Law with which we are dealing; for a little consideration will show us that we cannot impress two opposite suggestions at the same time. The man who tried to do so is described in the parable of the servant who threw his fellow-servant into prison after his own debt had been cancelled. The previous pardon availed him nothing, and he was cast into prison till he should pay the uttermost farthing.

The meaning becomes evident when we see that what we are dealing with is the supreme Law of our own being. We do not really believe what we do not act up to; if, therefore, we cast our fellow-servant into prison, no amount of philosophical speculation in an opposite direction will set us at liberty. Why? Because our action demonstrates that our real belief is in limitation. Such compulsion can only proceed from the idea that we shall be the poorer if we do not screw the money out of our fellow-servant, and this is to deny our own power of drawing from the Infinite in the most emphatic manner, and so to destroy the whole edifice of Liberty.

We cannot impress upon ourselves too strongly the impossibility of living by two contradictory principles at the same time. And the same argument holds good when we conceive that the debt is due to our injured feelings, our pride, and the like —the principle is always the same; it is that perfect Liberty places us above the reach of all such considerations, because by the very hypothesis of being absolute freedom, it can create far more rapidly than any of our fellow-servants can run up debts; and our attitude towards those who are thus running up scores should be to endeavor to lead them into that region of fulness where the relation of debtor and creditor cannot exist, because it becomes merged in the radiation of creative power.

But perhaps the most impressive of all the parables was that in which, on the night when He was betrayed, the Master expressed the great mystery of God and Man by symbolic action rather than by words, girding Himself with a towel and washing the disciples' feet. He assured Peter that though the meaning of this symbolic act was not apparent at the time, it should become clear later on.

A wonderful light is thrown on this dramatization of a great principle by comparing it with the Master's utterance in Luke 12:35–37. The idea of girding is very conspicuous in that parable. First, we are bidden to have our loins girded and our lights burning, like unto men that wait for their Lord. Then we are told that if the servants are found thus prepared, when the Lord does come *the positions will be reversed*, and He will make *them* sit down and will gird Himself and serve *them*.

Now what Jesus in this parable taught in words, He taught on the night of the Last Supper in acts. There is a strict parallel; in both cases the Master, the Lord, girds Himself and serves those who had hitherto accounted themselves His servants. The emphatic reduplication of this parable shows that here we have something of the very highest importance presented to us; and undoubtedly it is the veiled statement of the supreme mystery of individual being. And this mystery is the raising to the highest spiritual levels of the old maxim that Nature will obey us in proportion as we first obey Nature. This is the ordinary rule of all science. The universal principles can never act contrary to themselves, whether on the spiritual or the physical level, and therefore unless we are prepared by study of the Law and obedience to it, we cannot make use of these principles at any level; but granted such preparation on our part and the Law becomes our humble servant, obeying us in every particular on the one condition that we first obey it. It is thus that modern science has made us masters of a world of power which, for all practical purposes, did not exist in the times of the Tudors; and, transferring this truth to the highest and innermost, to the very Principle of Life itself, the meaning becomes plain. Because the Life-Principle is not something separate from ourselves, but is the Supporter of our individuality, therefore the more we understand and obey its great *generic* Law, the more fully shall we be able to make any *specific* applications of it that we like. But on one condition: we must be washed. "If I wash thee not, thou hast no part with Me" were the words of the Master. He spoke as the conscious mouthpiece of the Universal Spirit, and this must therefore be taken as the personal utterance of the Spirit itself; and seen in this light, the meaning becomes clear; we must first be cleansed by the Spirit.

And here we meet with another symbolical fact of the highest importance. This dramatization of the final truth of spiritual knoweldge took place after the supper was ended. Now as we all know, the supper was itself of supreme symbolical significance. It was the Jewish Passover and the Christian Commemoration, and tradition tells us it was also the symbolic act by which, throughout antiquity, the highest initiates signified their identical realization of Truth, however apparently separated by outward forms or nationality.

We find these mystical emblems of bread and wine presented to Abraham by Melchizedek, himself the type of the man who has realized the supreme truth of the birth which is "without father, without mother, without beginning of days or end of years";* and therefore if we would grasp the full meaning of the Master's action on that last night, we must understand the meaning of the symbolic meal of which He and His followers had just partaken. Briefly stated, it is the recognition by the participant of his unity with, and power of appropriating, the Divine in its twofold mode of Spirit and Substance.

Science and Religion are not two separate things. They both have the same object: to bring us nearer and nearer to the point where we shall find ourselves in touch with the ONE Universal Cause. Therefore the two were never dissociated by the greatest thinkers of antiquity, and the inseparable-

*Hebrews 7:3—*Ed.*

ness of energy and matter, which is now recognized by the most advanced science as the starting-point of all its speculations, is none other than the old, old doctrine of the identity of Spirit and ultimate Substance.

Now it is this twofold nature of the Universal First Cause that is symbolized by bread and wine. The fluid and the solid, or Spirit and Substance, as the two universal supports of all manifested Forms—these are the universal principles which the two typical elements signify. But in order that the individual may be consciously benefited by them, he must recognize his own participation in them, and he denotes his Knowledge on this point by eating the bread and drinking the wine; and his intention in so doing is to signify his recognition of two great facts: one, that he lives by continually drawing from the Infinite Spirit in its twofold unity; and the other, that he not only does this automatically but also has power to consciously differentiate the Universal Energy for any specific purpose that he will.

Now this combination of dependence and control could not be more perfectly symbolized than by the acts of eating and drinking. We cannot do without food, but it is at our own discretion to select what and when we shall eat. And if we realize the true meaning of "the Christ," we shall see that it is that principle of Perfected Humanity which is the highest expression of the Universal Spirit-Substance; and taken in this sense, the bread and wine are fitting emblems of the flesh and blood, or Substance and Spirit, of "the Son of Man," the ideal Type of all Humanity.

And so it is that we cannot realize the Eternal Life except by consciously partaking of the innermost Life-Principle, with due recognition of its true nature—not meaning the mere observance of a ceremonial rite, however august in its associations, and however useful as a powerful suggestion; but meaning personal recognition of the Supreme Truth which that rite signifies.

This, then, was the meaning of the symbolic meal which had just concluded. It indicated the participant's recognition of his union with the Universal Spirit as being the supreme fact on which his individual life was based, the ultimate of all Truth. Now the word rendered "washed" in John 13:10 is more correctly given in the Revised Version as "bathed," a word which signifies total immersion. But no "bathing" had taken place on this occasion; to what, then, did Jesus allude when He spoke to His disciples as men who had been "bathed"? It is precisely that which, in Ephesians 5:26, is spoken of as "the washing of water by the word," "water" being, as we have already seen, the Universal Substance, and "the word" the synonym for that Intelligence which is the very essence of Spirit. The meaning, then, is that by partaking of this symbolic meal they had signified their recognition of their own total immersion in the ONE Universal Divine Being, which is at once both Spirit and Substance; and since they could not conceive of It otherwise than as Most Holy, this recognition must thenceforward have a purifying influence upon the whole man.

This great recognition does not need to be repeated. Seen once, it is seen forever; and therefore "he that is washed needeth not save to wash his feet, but is clean every whit."* But though the principle is grasped—which, of course, is the substantial foundation of the new life—immediate perfection does not follow. Very far from it. And so we have to come day by day to the Spirit for the washing away of those stains which we contract in our daily walk through life. "If we say that we have no sin, the truth is not in us; but if we confess our sin, He is faithful and just to forgive us our sin and to cleanse us from all unrighteousness."†

It is this daily confession, not to man but to the Divine Spirit Itself, which produces the daily cleansing, and thus Its first service to us is to wash our feet. If we thus receive the daily washing, we

*The New American Standard Bible shows "He who has bathed needs only to wash his feet, but is completely clean" (John 13:10).—*Ed.*
†1 John 1:8,9—*Ed.*

shall, day by day, put away from us that sense of separation from the Divine Universal Mind which only the conscious retention of guilt in the heart can produce, after once we have been "bathed" by the recognition of our individual relation to It; and if our study of the Bible has taught us anything, it has taught us that the very Essence of Life is in its identity and unity throughout all forms of manifestation.

To allow ourselves, therefore, to remain conscious of separation from the Spirit of the Whole is to accept the idea of Disintegration, which is the very principle of death; and if we thus accept death at the fountainhead, it must necessarily spread through the whole stream of our individual existence and poison the waters. But it is inconceivable that anyone who has once realized the Great Unity should ever again willingly remain in conscious separation from it, and therefore immediate open-hearted approach to the Divine Spirit is the ever-ready remedy as soon as any consciousness of separation makes itself felt.

And the symbol includes yet another meaning. If the bathing or total immersion signifies our unity with the Spirit of the Whole, then the washing of the feet must signify the same thing in a lesser degree, and the meaning implied is the ever-present attendance of the Infinite Undifferentiated Spirit ready to be differentiated by us to any daily service, no matter how lowly. Seen in this light, this acted parable is not a mere reminder of our imperfection—which, unless corrected by a sense of power, could only be a perpetual suggestion of weakness that would incapacitate us from doing anything—but it indicates our continual command over all the resources of the Infinite for every object that all the endless succession of days can ever bring before us. We may draw from it what we like, when we like, and for what purpose we like; nothing can prevent us but ignorance or consciousness of separation.

The idea thus graphically set forth was expanded throughout that marvellous discourse with which the Master's ministry in His mortal body terminated. As ever, His theme was the perfect Liberty of the individual resulting from recognition of our true relation to the Universal Mind. The ONE great I AM is the Vine, the lesser ones are the branches. We cannot bear fruit except we abide in the Vine; but abiding in it, there is no limit to the developments we may attain.

The Spirit of Truth will guide us into *all* Truth, and the possession of all Truth must carry the possession of all Power along with it; and since the Spirit of Truth can be none other than the Spirit of Life, to be guided into all Truth must be to be guided into the Power of an endless life.

This does not need our removal from the world:

"I pray not that Thou shouldest take them out of the world, but that Thou shouldest keep them from the evil."* What is needed is ceasing to eat of that poisonous fruit the tasting of which expelled Man from the Paradise he is designed to inhabit. The true recognition of the ONE leaves no place for any other; and if we follow the Master's direction not to estimate things by their superficial appearance, but by their central principle of being, then we shall find that nothing is evil in essence, and that the origin of evil is always in a wrong application of what is good in itself, thus bringing us back to the declaration of the first chapter of Genesis, that God saw all that He had created, "and behold it was very good."

If, then, we realize that our Liberty resides in the creative power of our Thought, we shall see the immense importance of recognizing the essence of things as distinguished from the misplaced order in which we often first become acquainted with them. If we let our Thought dwell on an inverted order, we perpetuate that order; but if, going below the surface, we fix our Thought upon the essential nature of things and see that it is logically impossible for anything to be *essentially* bad which is a specific expression of the Universal Good, then we

*John 17:15—*Ed.*

shall in our Thought call all things good, and so help to bring about that golden age when the old inverted order shall have passed away, and a new world of joy and liberty shall take its place.

This, then, is briefly the line followed by the Master's teaching, and His miracles were simply the natural outcome of His perfect recognition of His own principles. Already the unfolding recognition of these principles is beginning to produce the same results at the present day, and the number of well-authenticated cures effected by mental means increases every year.* And this is precisely in accordance with Jesus' own prediction. He enumerated the signs which should follow those who really believed what He really taught, and in so saying He was simply making a statement of cause and effect. He never set up His power as proof of a nature different from our own; on the contrary, He said that those who learned what He taught should eventually be able to do still greater miracles, and He summed up the whole position in the words "the disciple when he is perfected shall be as his Master."†

Again, He laid special stress on the perfect naturalness of all that He taught by guarding us

*See footnote, p. 263—*Ed.*

†See Luke 6:40—*Ed.*

against the error of supposing that the intervention of any intermediary was required between us and "the Father." If we could assign such a position to any being, it would be to Himself; but He emphatically disclaims it. "In that day ye shall ask in My name; *and I say not unto you that I will pray the Father for you*, for the Father Himself loveth you, because ye have loved Me and believed that I came forth from the Father" (John 16:26,27). If the student has realized what has been said in the chapter on "the Sacred Name," he will see that the opening words of this utterance can be nothing else than a statement of universal Truth, and that the love and belief in Himself, spoken of in the concluding clause, are the love of this Truth exhibited in its highest form as Man evolved to perfection, and belief in the power of the Spirit to produce such an evolution.

I do not say that there is nothing personal in the statement; on the contrary, it is eminently personal to "the Man Christ Jesus," but as the Type of Perfected Humanity—the first-fruit of the further evolution which is to complete the pyramid of manifested being upon earth by the introduction of the Fifth Kingdom, which is that of the Spirit.

When we realize what is accomplished in Him, we see what is potential in ourselves; and since we have now reached the point beyond which any further evolution can only result from our conscious cooperation with the evolutionary principle, all our future progress depends on the extent to which we do recognize the potentialities contained in our own individuality.

Therefore, to realize the manifestation of the Divine which Jesus stands for, and to love it, is the indispensable condition for attaining that access to "the Father" which means the full development in ourselves of all the powers of the Spirit.

The point which rivets our attention in this utterance of the Master's is the fact that we do not need the intervention of any third party to beseech "the Father" for us, because "the Father" Himself loves us. This statement,* which we may well call the greatest of all the teachings of Jesus, setting us free, as it does, from the cramping influences of a limited and imperfect theology, He has bracketed together with the recognition of Himself; and therefore if we would follow His teaching, we cannot separate these two things which He has joined; but if we realize in Him the embodiment of the Divine Ideal of Humanity, His meaning becomes clear—it is that our recognition of this ideal is itself the very thing that places us in immediate touch with "the Father."

*I.e. John 16:26,27—*Ed.*

By accepting the Divine Ideal as our own, we *provide the conditions* under which the Undifferentiated Universal Subconscious Mind becomes able to differentiate Itself into the particular and concrete expression of that Potential of Personality which is eternally inherent in It; and thus in each one who realizes the Truth which the Master taught, the Universal Mind attains an individualization capable of consciously recognizing Itself.

To attain this is the great end of Evolution, and in thus gaining Its end the ONE becomes the MANY, and the MANY return into the ONE—not by an absorption depriving them of individual identity, which would be to stultify the entire operation of the Spirit in Evolution by simply ending where it had begun, but by impressing upon innumerable individualities the perfect and completed likeness of that Original in the *potential* image of which they were first created.

The entire Bible is the unfolding of its initial statement that Man is made in the image of God, and the teaching of Jesus is the proclamation and demonstration of this Truth in its complete development, the Individual rejoicing in perfect Life and Liberty because of his conscious ONE-ness with the Universal.

The teaching of Jesus, whether by word or deed, may therefore be summed up as follows. He says in effect to each of us: What you really are in essence is a concentration of the ONE Universal Life-Spirit into conscious Individuality. If you live from the recognition of this Truth as your starting-point, it makes you Free. You cannot do this so long as you imagine that you have one centre and the Infinite another. You can only do it by recognizing that the two centres coincide and that That which, as being Infinite, is incapable of centralization in Itself finds centre in you.*

Think of these things until you see that it is impossible for them to be otherwise, and then step forward in perfect confidence, knowing that the universal principles must necessarily act with the same mathematical precision in yourself that they do in the attractions of matter or in the vibrations of ether. His teaching is identical with the teaching of Moses, that there is only ONE Being anywhere, and that the various degrees of its manifested consciousness are to be measured by one standard—the recognition of the meaning of the words I AM.

I have endeavored to show that the Bible is neither a collection of traditions belonging only to

*For Troward's only known spiritual mind treatment, which is based on this concept, see *The Edinburgh & Doré Lectures*, p. 137, last par. (DeVorss ed'n; pp. 26, 27 of earlier ed'ns of *Doré Lectures*).—*Ed.*

a petty tribe, nor yet a statement of dogmas which can give no account of themselves beyond the protestation that they are mysteries which must be accepted by faith—which faith, when we come to analyze it, consists only in accepting the bare assertion of those very persons who, when we ask them for the explanation of the things they bid us believe, are unable to give any explanation beyond the word "MYSTERY."

The true element of Mystery we shall never get rid of, for it is inherent in the ultimate nature of all things; but it is an element that perpetually unfolds, inviting us at each step to still further inquiry by satisfactorily and intelligently answering every question that we put in really logical succession, and thus the Mystery continually opens out into Meaning and never pulls us up short with an anathema for our irreverence in daring to inquire into Divine secrets.

When the interrogated is driven to the fulmination of anathemas, it is very plain that he has reached the end of his tether. As Byron says in "Don Juan":

> He knew not what to say, and so he swore.

and therefore this mode of answering a question always indicates one of two things: ignorance of the subject or intentional concealment of facts; and on either alternative, any "authority" which thus only tells us to "shut up" thereby at once loses all claim to our regard. Every undiscovered fact in the great Universal Order is a Divine Secret until we find the key that unlocks it; but the Psalmist tells us that the secret of the Lord is with them that fear Him, and the Master says that there is nothing hidden that shall not be revealed.

To seek, therefore, to understand the great principles on which it is written, so far from being an act of presumption, is the most practical proof we can give of our reverence for the Sacred Volume; and if the foregoing pages have in any way helped the reader to see in the Bible a statement of the working of Laws which are inherent in the nature of things and follow an intelligible sequence of cause and effect, my purpose in writing will be answered.

The limited space at my disposal has allowed me only to treat the whole subject in an introductory manner, and in particular I have not yet shown the method by which the ONE Universal Principle follows out an *exclusive* line of unfoldment, building up a "Chosen People" by a process of *natural selection* culminating in the Great Central Figure of the Gospels. It does this without in any way departing from its *universal* character, for it is that Power which cannot deny itself; but it does it as a consequence of this very universality; and upon the importance of this specialized action of the Universal Principle to the future development of the race it is impossible to lay too much stress.

The Bible tells us that there is such a special selection, and if we have found truth in its more general statements, we may reasonably expect to find the same truth in its more specialized statements also.

CHAPTER 11

The Forgiveness of Sin

In the preceding chapters I have dealt principally with the teaching of the Bible regarding the *reciprocity* of being between God and man—that ultimate spiritual nature of man which affords the *generic* basis in *all* men upon which the Spirit of God can work to produce the further *specific* development of the individual. But if we stop short at the recognition of this merely generic similarity, we are liable to be led into an erroneous course of reasoning resulting in logical conclusions the very opposite of all that the Bible is seeking to teach us; in a word, we shall be led into an atheism far deeper than that of the mere materialist, in that it is on the spiritual plane—the inverted development of the supreme principle of our nature.

Such a dire result comes from a one-sided view of things, a knowledge of certain truths without the knowledge of their counterbalancing truths; and the counterbalancing truth which will preserve us from so great a calamity is contained in the Bible teaching regarding the forgiveness of sin.

Once grant that there is such a thing as the forgiveness of sin, and the root of all possible spiritual inversion is logically cut away, for then there must be One who is able and willing to forgive, and who is therefore the object of worship and is capable of entering into a specific, conscious, personal relation to us. It is therefore important to realize what the Bible teaching on this subject is.

The logic of it is sufficiently simple if we grant the premises on which it starts. It is that man, by his essential and true innermost nature, is a being fitted and intended to live in uninterrupted intercourse with the All-creating Spirit, thus continually receiving a ceaseless inflow of life from this infinite source. At the same time, it is impossible for a being capable of thus partaking of the infinite life of the Originating Spirit to be a mere piece of mechanism, mechanically incapable of moving in more than one direction; for if he is to reproduce in his individuality that power of origination and initiative which must be the very essence of the Creative Spirit's recognition of itself, he must possess a corresponding liberty of choice as to the way in which he will use his powers; and if he chooses wrongly, the inevitable law of cause and effect must produce the natural consequences of his choice.

The nature of this wrong choice is told us in the allegorical story of "the Fall." It is mistaking the sequence of laws which necessarily proceeds from any creative act for the creative power itself—the error of looking upon secondary causes as the originating cause and not seeing that they are themselves effects of something antecedent which works through them to the production of the ultimate effect. This is the fundamental error, and the opposite truth consists in connecting the ultimate effect intended *directly* with the intention of the originating intelligence and (from this point of view) excluding all consideration of the chain of intermediary causes which links these two extremes together.

The exact weighing and balancing and calculating of the action of secondary causes, or particular laws of *relation*, has its proper place; it is the necessary basis of our work when we are *constructing* anything *from without*, just as an architect could not build a safe house without carefully calculating the strains and thrusts to which his materials would be subjected. But when we are considering an act of *creation*, we are dealing with an exactly opposite process, one that works *from within* by a *vital growth* which naturally assimilates to itself all that is necessary for its completion.

In the latter case we do not have to consider the

mechanism through which the vital energy brings forth its ultimate fruition, for by the very fact of its being inherent energy working for manifestation in a certain direction, it must necessarily produce all those relations, visible or invisible, which go to make the completed whole.

The fundamental error consists in ignoring this distinction between *direct creation* and external construction—in entirely losing sight of the former and consequently attempting to accomplish by knowledge of particular laws, which are applicable only to construction from without, what can only be accomplished by a direct creation which produces laws instead of being restricted by them.

The temptation, then, is to substitute our intellectual knowledge of the relations between various existing laws with which we are acquainted for that Creative Power which is not subject to any antecedent conditions and can produce what it will, while conforming always to its own recognition of itself as perfectly harmonious Being.* This temptation is a very subtle one. It appeals to our intellect. It appeals to all that we can gather from secondary causes, whether in the seen or the unseen, and to all the deductions we can make from these observations. To all appearances it is so entirely reason-

*See my *Creative Process in the Individual.*

able, only its reasoning is restricted to the circle of secondary causation and contemplates the great First Cause as a mere force whose action is limited by certain particular laws.

Looked at superficially, it does appear as if this course of reasoning was correct. But in truth it does not take into account the *originating* power of the Creative Spirit and is in reality a course of reasoning which is only applicable to construction from without and not to growth from within.

Now so long as we do not recognize a Power which can transcend all our past experiences, we naturally look to a more extended knowledge of particular laws as a means by which we can attain to a power of control which will at last place us beyond subjection to any control, the general principle involved being that by our knowledge we can balance the positive and negative aspects of law against each other in any proportion we like and become masters of the situation by this method.

Is not this a correct description of much of the teaching we meet with at the present day? and does it not exactly agree with the words of the old allegory, "ye shall be as gods knowing good and evil"?*

The ultimate desire of every human being is for more fulness of life — to thoroughly enjoy living —

*Genesis 3:5 — *Ed.*

and the more we enjoy living, the more we shall naturally desire to live and to enjoy living still more. In a word, our true desire, under whatever disguises we may try to conceal it, is to "have life and to have it more abundantly."* This desire is innate in us because of our *generic* relation to the Spirit of Life, and therefore, so far from being condemned by Scripture, its fulfillment is placed before us as the one object of attainment, and the professed purpose of the Bible is to lead us to seek it in the right way instead of in the wrong one. To seek it in the right way is Righteousness or Rightness. To seek it in the wrong way is the Inversion of Rightness and is what is meant by Sin.

Those grosser forms of sin which we all recognize as such are only the one original transgression—of seeking from without what can only come by growth from within—when assuming its crudest aspect; but the underlying principle is the same; and so the allegory of the Fall is typical of all sin, of that inverted conception of life which, because it is inverted, must necessarily lead us away from the Spiritual Source of Life instead of towards it. The story is, so to say, a sort of algebraical generalization of the factors concerned.

When this becomes clear to us, we begin to see

*John 10:10—*Ed.*

the necessity for the removal of sin. We see that hitherto we have been trying to live by an inverted conception of the principle of Life, whether this wrong conception has shown itself in crude and gross forms or more subtly in the purely intellectual region.

In either case the result is the same—the consciousness that we have not free intercourse with the Spiritual Source of Life; and as this dawns upon us, we instinctively feel the need of some other way than the one we have been hitherto pursuing. We find that what we want is not Knowledge but Love. And this is logical, for in the last analysis we shall find that Love is the only Creative Power.*

Then we perceive that what we require for the perpetuation and continual increase of our individual life is a mental attitude which renders us perpetually and increasingly receptive of the Creative Love—the consciousness of a personal and individual relation to it beyond, and in addition to, our merely generic relation as items in the cosmic whole.

Then something must be done to assure us of this specific relation, to assure us that neither our erroneous thoughts in the past, nor yet the erroneous action to which they have given rise, can separate

*See *The Creative Process in the Individual.*

us from this Love, either by making it turn away from us, or by a law of cause and effect proceeding from our wrong thoughts and acts themselves. And to give us such a confidence we require to be assured that the initiative movement proceeds from the side of the Divine Spirit; for if we suppose that the initiative starts from *our* side, then we can have no assurance that it has been accepted, or that the law of "Karma" is not dogging our steps.

It is this misconception of pacifying the Almighty by an initiative originating on *our* side that shows itself in penances, sacrifices, and various rites and ceremonies at the end of which we do not know whether our operations have been successful, or whether through deficiency in quantity or quality they have failed of the desired result.

All such performances are vitiated by the inherent defect of making the first move towards reconciliation come from *our* side. It is nothing else than carrying into our highest spiritual yearnings the old error of trying to produce by working from without what can only be produced by growth from within. We are still substituting the constructive process for the creative.

Accordingly, the Bible tells us that the fundamental proposition that there is such a thing as forgiveness of sin is enunciated by God Himself; and so we find that the story of the Fall includes the promise of One by whom man shall be redeemed and released from sin and brought into conscious realization of that reciprocal intercourse with the Source of Life which is the essence of his innermost being. Man is told to look to the Divine promise of forgiveness, and from this point onwards belief in this promise is set forth as the way by which sin and its consequences are effectually removed.

I sometimes meet with those who object to the teaching that there is forgiveness. To such I would say, Why do you object to this teaching? Of course, if you are entirely without sin, you have no need of it for yourself; but then you are a very rare exception and at the same time beastly selfish not to consider all the rest of us who are of the more ordinary sort. Or if you put it that everybody is without sin, then the newspapers of all countries flatly contradict you with their daily details of thefts, murders, swindles, and the like.

But perhaps you will say that sin must be punished. Why *must*? What is the object of punishment? Its purpose is to rub it well in, so that the offender may not do it again for fear of consequences. But supposing he has become convinced of the true nature of his offence so as to hate it for its own sake and to shrink from it with abhorrence, what then is to be gained by going on whacking him? The change in his own view of things has already accomplished all, and more than all, that any amount of whacking could do, and this is the teaching of the Bible. Its purpose is to see sin in its true light as severance from the Source of Life, and if this has been accomplished why should punishment be prolonged?

Again, the conception of a God who *will* not forgive sin when repented of is the conception of a monstrosity. It is the conception of the Spirit of Life determining to deal death, when by its very nature it must be seeking to express Life to the fullest extent that the expressing vehicle will admit of; and repentance is turning away from something that had previously hindered this fuller expression. Therefore such a conception is illogical, for it implies the Spirit of Life acting in opposition to itself. Also such a God ceases to be the object of worship, for there is nothing to be gained by worshiping Him. He can only be the object of our fear and hatred.

On the other hand, the conception of a God who *cannot* forgive sin is the conception of no God at all. It is the conception of a mere Force, and you cannot enter into a personal relation with unintelligent forces—you can only study them scientifically and utilize them so far as your knowledge of their law admits; and this logically brings you back to your own knowledge and power as your only source of life, so that in this case also there is nothing to worship.

If, then, there is such a mental attitude as that of worship, the looking to an Infinite Source of life and joy and strength, it can only be based upon the recognition that this All-creating Spirit is able to forgive sin and desires to do so.

We may therefore say that the conception of itself as pardoning all who ask for pardon is necessarily an integral portion of the Spirit's Self-recognition in its relation to the human race, and the inherentness of this idea is set forth in Scripture in such phrases as "the Lamb of God that taketh away the sin of the world" and "the Lamb slain from the foundation of the world," thus pointing to an aspect of the Spirit's Self-contemplation exactly reciprocal to the need of all who desire to be set free from that inversion of their true nature which, while it continues, must necessarily prevent their unimpeded access to the Spirit of Life.

Then, since the Divine Self-conception is bound to work out into realization, a supreme manifestation of this eternal principle is the legitimate outcome of all that we can conceive of the creative working of the Spirit when viewed from the particular standpoint of the existence of sin in the world, and so the appearing of One who should give complete expression in space and time to the Spirit's recognition of human needs by a supreme act of self-sacrificing Love reasonably forms the grand centre of the whole teaching of the Bible.

The Great Sacrifice is the Self-offering of Love to meet the requirements of the soul of man. Our psychological constitution requires it, and it is adequately adapted to fit in with every aspect of our mental nature, whether in the least or the most advanced members of the race. It is the supreme manifestation of that Love which is the Original Creative Power, and the Bible presents it to us as such.

Hear Christ's own description of it: "Greater love hath no man than this, that a man lay down his life for his friends"; "God so loved the world that He sent His only begotten Son into the world, that whosoever believeth on Him should not perish but should have everlasting life."

All is attributed to Love on the one hand and Belief on the other—the Creating Spirit and the simple reception of it—thus meeting exactly those conditions which we found to constitute the conditions for vital growth from within as distinguished from mechanical construction from without, and therefore not depending on our knowledge but on our faith.

Nor is this conception of the forgivingness of the All-originating Love to be found in the New Testament only. If we turn to the Old Testament we find such statements as the following: "And the Lord descended in a cloud and stood with him [Moses] there, and proclaimed the Name of the Lord. And the Lord passed by and proclaimed, The Lord, the Lord God, merciful and gracious, long-suffering and abundant in goodness and truth, keeping mercy for thousands, forgiving iniquity, transgression, and sin" (Ex. 34:5–7). "I, even I, am he that blotteth out thy transgressions *for my own sake*, and will not remember thy sins" (Isaiah 43:25). "I have blotted out as a thick cloud thy transgressions, and as a cloud thy sins; return unto me, for I have redeemed thee" (Isaiah 44:22). "If the wicked will turn from all his sins that he hath committed, and keep all my statutes, and do that which is lawful and right, he shall surely live, he shall not die. All his transgressions that he hath committed, they shall not be mentioned unto him; in his righteousness that he hath done he shall live" (Ezek. 18:21,22).

No doubt on the other hand there are threatenings against sin; but the whole tenor of the Bible is clear, that these threatenings apply only so long as we continue to do evil. Both the promises and the threatenings are nothing else than the statement of that Law of Correspondence with which my readers are no doubt sufficiently familiar—the great creative law by which spiritual causes produce their analogues in the outer world, and which is identically the same law whether it works positively or negatively.

The phrase "for my own sake," in Isaiah 43:25, should be noted, as it exactly bears out what I have said about the inherent quality of forgiveness as forming a necessary part of the Creating Spirit's conception of itself in its relation to the human race. This is the fundamental basis of the whole matter, and this truth has been dimly perceived by all the great religions of the world; in fact, it is just the perception of this truth that distinguishes a *religion* from a mere philosophy on the one hand and from magical rites on the other; and I think I cannot end this chapter more suitably than by a quotation which shows how, ages before Christianity was known to them, our rude Norse ancestors had at least some adumbration that the supreme offering must be that of the Divine Love to itself. The passage occurs in the Elder Edda, where O-din, the Supreme God, addresses himself while hanging in self-sacrifice in Vgdrasil, the Cosmic Tree:

I knew that I hung
In the wind-rocked tree
Nine whole nights,
Wounded with a spear,

And to O-din offered,
Myself to myself,
On that tree
Of which no one knows
From what root it springs.

(From *Strange Survivals*, by Baring-Gould)*

*Sabine Baring-Gould (1834–1924), English clergyman and author—*Ed.*

CHAPTER 12

Forgiveness

ITS RELATION TO HEALING AND TO THE STATE OF THE DEPARTED IN THE OTHER WORLD

IF WE have now grasped some conception of forgiveness as one of the essential qualities of the All-creating Spirit, it will throw some light on several occasions when Jesus accompanied His miracles of healing with the words "Thy sins are forgiven."

There must have been some intimate connection between the forgiveness and the healing, and though the exact nature of this connection may be beyond our present perception, involving relations of cause and effect too deep for our imperfect powers of analysis, still we can see in a general way that it is in accordance with the teaching of the Bible on the subject.

The Bible is a book about man in his relation to God, and it therefore starts with certain fundamental statements regarding this relation. These are to the effect that death, and consequently disease and decrepitude, are not laws of man's innermost being. How *could* they be? How could the negative be the law of the positive? How could death be the law of Life? Therefore we are told that in the true order of things this is not the case.

The first thing we are told about man is that he is made in the image and likeness of God, the Spirit of Life, therefore capable of manifesting a similar equality of Life. But we must note the words "image" and "likeness." They do not impart identity but resemblance. An "image" implies an original to which it conforms, and so does a "likeness." These words remind us of the passage in which St. Paul speaks of our "reflecting as a mirror the glory of the Lord" and being thus "transformed into the same image from glory to glory" (2 Cor. 3:18, R.V.). It is this same idea as in the first chapter of Genesis, only expanded so as to show the method by which the image and likeness are produced. It is by Reflection. Our mind is, as it were, a mirror reflecting that towards which it is turned. This is the nature of Mind.

We become like what we contemplate. We cannot avoid it, for we are made that way, and therefore everything depends on what we are in the habit of contemplating. Then if we realize that growth, or the manifestation of the spiritual principle, always proceeds from the innermost to the outermost, by a creative process from within as distinguished from a constructive process from without, we shall see that the working of the mind upon the body, and the effect it will produce upon it, depends entirely on what form the mind itself is taking; and what form it will take depends on what it is reflecting.

This is the key to the great enigma. In proportion as we reflect the Pure Spirit of Life, we live; and in proportion as we reflect the Material, contemplating it as a power in itself instead of as the plastic vehicle of the Spirit, we bring ourselves under a law of limitation which culminates in death. It is the same law of Mind in both cases, only in the one case it is employed positively and in the other negatively.

Something like this seems to be St. Paul's idea when he says that the Law of the Spirit of Life makes him free from the law of sin and death (Rom. 8:2). It is always this law of mental reflection that is at work within us, producing its logical effects, positively or negatively, according to the image which it mirrors forth.

At the risk of appearing tedious, I may dwell for a while on the word "image." It is the substantive corresponding to the verb "to image"—that is, to fashion an "image" or "thought-form" by our mental power of imagery.

Now as I have endeavored to make clear in my book *The Creative Process in the Individual*, the life and substance of all things must first subsist as images in the Divine Mind before they can come into manifestation in the world of time and space, much as in Plato's conception of archetypal ideas; therefore we may read the text in Genesis as indicating that Man exists primarily in the Divine conception of him. The real, true Man subsists eternally in the Divine Imagination as the necessary correlative to the Spirit's Self-recognition as all that constitutes Personality.

If the Universal Spirit is to realize in itself the consciousness of Will, the perception of Beauty, and the reciprocity of Love—all, in fact, that makes life intelligently living—it can do so only by projecting a mental image which will give rise to the corresponding consciousness; and so we may read the text as meaning that Man thus subsists in the Divine image, or creating thought, of him. If the reader grasps this idea, he will find it throws light upon many otherwise perplexing problems.

This, then, is the real nature of sin. Whatever shape it may take, its essence is always the same: it is turning our mental mirror the wrong way and so reflecting the limited and negative, that which is not Life-in-itself, and consequently forming ourselves into a corresponding image and likeness.

The story of the Fall typifies the essential quality of *all* sin. It is seeking the Living among the dead—trying to build up the skill and power of the worker out of the atoms of the material in which he works; just as though, when you wanted a carpenter, you went into his workshop and tried to make him out of the sawdust.

Now if we grasp the great fundamental law that our mind, meaning by this our spiritual creative power, attracts conditions which correspond to its own conception of itself, and that its conception of itself must always be the exact reflection of its own dominant thought, then we can in some measure understand why Christ announced forgiveness of sin as the accompaniment of physical healing.

By sin, in the sense we have now seen, death and all lesser evils enter into the world. Sin is the cause and they are the effect. Then if the cause is removed, the effect must cease—the root of the plant has been cut away, and so the fruit must wither. It is a simple working of cause and effect.

It is true that Jesus is not recorded to have announced forgiveness in every case in which he bestowed healing, and no doubt he had as good reasons for not making the announcement in some cases as for making it in others.

I cannot pretend to analyze those reasons, for that would imply a knowledge on my part equal to his own; but from what we do know of pyschological laws and of the power of mind over body, I might hazard the conjecture that in those cases where he pronounced forgiveness, the sufferer apprehended that his sickness was in some way the consequence of his sins, and therefore it was necessary to his bodily healing that he should be assured of their pardon.

In other cases there may not have been such a conviction, and to speak of forgiveness would only withdraw the mind of the sufferer from that immediately receptive attitude which was necessary for the working of the spiritual power.

But who shall say that the principle of the removal of the root of suffering by the forgiveness of sin was not always present in the mind of the august Healer? Rather we may suppose that it always was.

On one occasion he very pointedly put this forward. The proof, he said, that the Son of Man has power on earth to forgive sins is this, I can say to this palsied man, "Arise and walk," and it is accomplished (Luke 5:24). This was what was in the mind of the Great Healer, and comparing it with the general teaching of Scripture on the subject, we may reasonably suppose that he always worked from this basic principle, whether the exigencies of the particular case made it, or not, to impress the fact of forgiveness upon the person to be healed.

If we start with the assumption that sickness and death of the body result from imperfect realization of life by the soul, and that the extent and mode of the soul's realization of life is the result of the extent and mode of its realization of union with its Divine Source, then it follows that the logical root of healing must be in the removal of the sense of separation—the removal, that is, of that inverted conception of our relation to the Spirit of Life which is "sin"—and the replacing of it by the right conception in accordance with which we shall more and more fully reflect the true image of "the Father" or Parent Spirit.

When we see this, we begin to apprehend more clearly the meaning of St. Paul's words "There is now no condemnation to them that are in Christ Jesus, which walk not after the flesh but after the Spirit."*

Again, there is another phase of this subject which we cannot afford to neglect. Although, as it appears to me, there are grounds for supposing that the *present* resurrection of the body—its transmutation while in the present life into a body of another order, like to the resurrection body of

*Romans 8:1—*Ed.*

Christ—is not beyond the bounds of possibility, still this supreme victory of the Life-Principle is not a thing of general realization; and so we are confronted by the question, What happens on the other side when we get there? I have treated this question at some length in my *Creative Process in the Individual*, but I would here refer to it chiefly in connection with the subject of the forgiveness of sin.

Now if, as I apprehend, the condition of consciousness when we pass out of the body is in the majority of cases purely subjective, then from what we know of the laws of subjective mind we may infer that we live there in the consciousness of whatever was our dominant mode of thought during earth life.

We have brought this over with us on parting with our objective mentality as it operates through its physical instrument, the brain; and if this is the case, then the nature of our experiences in the other world will depend on the nature of the dominant thought with which we have left this one, the idea which was most deeply impressed upon our subjective mind.

If this be so, what a stupendous importance it gives to the question whether we do or do not believe in the forgiveness of sin. If we pass into the unseen with the fixed idea that no such thing is possible, then what can our subjective experience be but the bearing of a burden of which we can find no way to rid ourselves; for by the conditions of the case, all those objective things with which we can now distract our attention will be beyond our reach.

When the loss of our objective mentality deprives us of the power of inaugurating fresh trains of ideas, which practically means new outlooks upon life, we shall find ourselves bound within the memories of our past life on earth, and since the outward conditions which then colored our view of things will no longer exist, we shall see the motives and feelings which led to our actions in their true light, making us see what it was *in ourselves* rather than in our circumstances which led us to do as we did.

The mode of thought which gave the key to our past life will still be there, and no doubt the memory of particular facts also, for this is what has been most deeply impressed upon our subjective mind; and since by the conditions of the case the consciousness is entirely subjective, these memories will appear to be the reenacting of past things, only now seen in their true nature, stripped of all the accessories which gave a false coloring to them.

Of course what the pain of such a compulsory reenacting of the past life may amount to must depend on what the past life has been; but even in the most blameless life we can well suppose that there have been passages which we would rather not repeat when we saw the mental conditions in ourselves which gave rise to them—not necessarily crimes or grave moral delinquencies, but the shortcomings of the everyday respectable life, the unkind words we thought so little of but which cut so deep, the selfishness which perhaps ran on for years and which, because of that very self-centeredness, we did not see dimming the happiness of those around us. These and the like things of even the most blameless life we should not like to be compelled to repeat when seen in their true light, and how much less the episodes of a life which has not been blameless.

That there should be such a reenacting of past memories is what we might infer from our knowledge of the law of subjective mind, but there are not wanting certain facts of experience which go to support the *a priori* argument.*

Many of my readers, I daresay, will smile at the mention of ghosts, but I can assure them there is a good deal of reality in ghosts, especially *to the ghosts themselves.* Remember that if there are such things as ghosts, they were once people such as you

*Argument from self-evident propositions—*Ed.*

and I are today; and the practical point is that the reader may be a ghost himself before very long. Therefore one of my objects in the present chapter is to show how to avoid becoming a ghost.

I used to laugh at ghosts when I was a young man and thought it all bunkum, but an experience which I went through many years ago entirely changed my ideas on the subject and indeed was the starting-point of my giving consideration to the laws of the unseen side of things. If it had not been for that ghost, you would not be reading this book. However, I will not go into the details here, for the story has already been published both in French and English magazines.*

Of course, I don't believe everything I hear, nor do I think that because a thing is in print it is necessarily true—heaven forbid, for then how could I read the daily papers?—but applying to each case the rules of evidence as strictly as though I were trying a man for his life, I find a residuum of instances in which it is impossible to come to any other conclusion than that a haunting spirit has actually been seen.

We are often told that you never meet persons who have themselves seen a ghost but only those who

*See Ch. 2, "Some Psychic Experiences," of Troward's *The Law and the Word.—Ed.*

know somebody else who has; in other words, you can never get at the actual witness to cross-examine him, but only at hearsay evidence. But I can contradict this entirely.

Since I began to investigate the subject seriously, I am surprised at the number of persons of both sexes who have circumstantially related to me their personal experiences of this sort and have stood the test of careful cross-examination in which I held a brief for the standpoint of "scientific doubt." Therefore when I say a few words about ghosts, I am talking on a subject that I have investigated.

In a large majority of cases it will be found that the spirit appears to be bound to a particular spot and to go on repeating certain actions, and the inference is that the subjective dreaming, so to say, of the departed is in these cases so intense as to create a thought-form of their conception of themselves sufficiently vivid to impress itself upon the etheric atmosphere of the locality and so become visible to those who are sufficiently sensitive.

Now, that this is not always the consequence of some great crime or other terrible happening is shown by a case in which the former owners of a house, husband and wife, after having long been habitually seen about the premises, were at last questioned by a lady who was sufficiently sensitive to communicate with them. They stated that the only thing that bound them to the house was their inordinate love of it during life. They had so centered their minds upon it that now they could not get away though they longed to do so; and, judging by their appearance and the confirmation of their identity subsequently obtained from some old documents, it would seem that they had been tied up like this for several generations.

This is an instance of having rather too much of a "pied-à-terre,"* and I don't think any of us would like it to become our own case; and *a fortiori*† the same must hold good where the recollections of the departed are of a darker kind.

What, then, is the way out of the dilemma? It must be by some working of the law of cause and effect, and this working must take place somewhere within our own mind—we must in some way get a state of consciousness which will set us free from all troubling memories and keep before us, even in the unseen world, the prospect of happier developments.

Then the only mental attitude which can produce this effect is belief in forgiveness, the assurance that all the transgressions and shortcomings

*French, "foot to the ground"; a reference to a (usually temporary or secondary) dwelling-place—*Ed.*
†In the sense "all the more so"—*Ed.*

of the past have been blotted out forever. If we attain this realization in this present life, if this assurance is our dominant idea—the idea upon which all our other ideas are based—then by all the laws of mind we are bound to carry this consciousness with us into the other world and thus find ourselves free from all that would make our existence there unhappy.

Or even if we have not yet attained such a vivid assurance as to be able to say "I know," and can as yet only say "I hope," still the fact that we recognize that the *principle* of forgiveness exists will cause us to lay hold of it as our dominant idea in the subjective state and so place us in a position to gain clearer and clearer perception of the truth that there *is* forgiveness, and that it is *for us*.

Perhaps the critical reader may here remark that I am attributing to the subjective mind the power of starting a new train of ideas, and so contradicting what I have just said about the departed being shut up within the circle of those ideas which they have brought over with them from this world. It looks as if I had made a slip, but I haven't; for if we have carried over with us not perhaps the full assurance of actual pardon, but even the belief that forgiveness is possible, we have brought along with us a root idea whose very essence is that of making a new start.

It is the fundamental conception of a new order and as such carries with it the conception of ourselves as entering upon new trains of thought and new fields of action—in a word, the dominant idea of the subjective mind is that of having brought the objective mental faculties along with it. If this is the mode of self-consciousness then it becomes an actual fact, and the *whole* mentality is brought over in its entirety; so that those who are thus in the light are liberated from imprisonment within the circulus of past memories by the very same law which binds those fast who refuse to admit the liberating principle of forgiveness.*

It is the same law of our mental constitution in both cases, only acting affirmatively in the one and negatively in the other, just as an iron ship floats by the identical law by which a solid lump of iron sinks.

Of course we may conceive of degrees in these things. We may well suppose that some may recognize the actual working of forgiveness in their own case less clearly than others; but whatever may be the degree of recognition of the personal fact, the realization of the *principle* is the same for all; and this principle must assuredly bear fruit in due time

*See Ch. 8, "The Dénouement of the Creative Process," of Troward's *The Creative Process in the Individual*, especially pp. 85–103 (DeVorss ed'n; pp. 95–116 of earlier ed'ns).—*Ed.*

in the complete deliverance of the soul from all that would otherwise hold it in bondage.

Far be it from me to say that the case of those who pass over convinced in their denial of the principle of forgiveness is forever hopeless; but by the nature of mental law they must remain bound until they see it. Moreover by their denial of this principle they must fail to bring over their objective mentality, and so they must remain shut up in the world of their subjective memories until some of those who have brought over their *whole* mentality are able to penetrate the spheres of their subjective mind and impress upon it a new conception, that of forgiveness, and so plant in them the seed for the new growth of their objective mental powers.

And perhaps we may even go so far as to suppose that the power of those who are thus in wholeness of mind to aid those who are not is not confined to such as have passed over; it may be the privilege also of those who are still in the body, for the action of mind upon mind is not a thing of physical substances. If so, then we can see a reason for prayers for the departed, to say nothing of the many instances in which ghosts are reported to have besought the intercession of the living for their liberation. There is, however, in certain quarters a lamentable inversion of this principle where prayers for the departed are turned into an article of traffic and a means of making money. I may have something to say about this in another book, and meanwhile I would only say, Beware of spurious imitations.

Of course this picture of the condition of souls in the other world does not profess to be drawn from actual knowledge, but it appears to me to be a reasonable deduction from all that we know of the laws of our mental constitution; and if the experiences of the departed logically result from the working of those laws, then what greater action of the Divine Love and Wisdom can we conceive than such an expression of itself as must utilize these laws affirmatively for our liberation instead of negatively for our bondage? The law of Cause and Effect cannot be broken, but it can be applied with intelligence and love instead of being left to work itself out negatively for want of guidance.

So it is, then, that the doctrine of the forgiveness of sins is the mainspring of the Bible—the promise of a Messiah in the old Testament and the fulfillment of that promise in the New—and the realization, whether in or out of the body, that God is both able and desiring to forgive, freely and without any offering save that of his own providing, and requiring nothing in return except this: that "to whom much hath been forgiven, the same loveth much."

CHAPTER 13

THE DIVINE GIVING

IN THE last two chapters we have considered the principle of the forgiveness of sin, and having laid this foundation, I would now direct attention to the working of the same principle in other directions. In its essence it is the Quality of Givingness—Free Giving, having Simple Accepting for its correlative, for the clear reason that you cannot put a man in possession of a gift if he will not take it. Now a little consideration will show us that Free Givingness is a necessity of the very being of the All-originating Spirit. By the very fact that it is All-originating we have nothing to give to it, nothing except that reciprocity of feeling which, as we have seen, is fundamental to the Divine ideal of Man, that ideal which has called the human race into existence.

If, then, we have nothing to *give* but our love and worship, why not take up the position of grateful and expectant *receivers*? It simplifies matters and relieves us of a great deal of worry, and moreover it is undoubtedly scriptural. The reason we don't do so is because we don't believe in the free givingness, and consequently we cannot adopt a mental attitude of receiving, and so the Spirit cannot make the gift.

If we seek the reason why this is so, we shall find it in our materialism, our inability to see beyond secondary causes. We get things through certain visible channels, and we mistake these for the source.

"The things I possess I got with my money, and my money I got by my work." Of course you did. God doesn't put dollar bills or banknotes into your cash box by a conjuring trick. God makes things *generically,* whether it be iron or brains, and then we have to use them. But the iron or the brains, or whatever else it may be, ultimately proceeds from the All-creating Spirit; and the more clearly we see this, the easier we shall find it to go direct to the Spirit for all we want.

Then we shall argue that, just as the Spirit can create the thing we desire, so it can also create *the way* by which that thing shall come to us, and so we shall not be bothered about the way. We shall work according to the sort of abilities God has bestowed upon us and according to the opportunities provided; but we shall not try to force circumstances or to do something out of our line.

Then we shall find circumstances open out and our abilities increase, and this without putting any undue strain upon ourselves, but on the contrary with a great sense of restfulness.

And the secret is this: we are not bearing the burden ourselves. We are not trying to force things on the external plane by our objective powers, nor yet on the subjective plane by trying to compel the Spirit; therefore, though diligent in our calling, we are at rest. And the foundation of this rest is that we believe in a Divine Promise, and the Promise is in the nature of the Divine Being.

This is why the Bible lays so much stress upon the idea of Promise. Promise is the law of Creative Power simplified to the utmost simplicity. Faith in a Divine Promise is the strongest attitude of mental Affirmation. It is the affirmation of the *desire* of the Creative Spirit to create the gift, and of its power and willingness to do so, and therefore of the production also of all the means by which the gift is to be brought to us. Also it fixes no limits and so does not restrict the mode of operation, and thus it conforms exactly to the principles of the original cosmic creation, so that the whole universe around us becomes a testimony to the stability of the foundation on which our hope is based. This reference to the cosmic creation as bearing witness to the ground of our faith is of constant recurrence in the Bible, and its purpose is to impress upon us that the Power to which we look is that Power which in the beginning made the heavens and the earth.

The reason why this is made the starting-point of faith is that we start with an undoubted fact: the universe exists. Then a little consideration will show us that it must have had its origin in the Thought of the Universal Spirit before its manifestation in time and space, so that here we start with another self-evident fact; and these two obvious and incontrovertible facts supply us with premises from which to reason; so that knowing our premises to be true, we know that our conclusion must be true also, if we only reason correctly from the premises. This is the logic of it.

Then the reasoning proceeds as follows: in the beginning there were no antecedent conditions, and the whole creation came out of the desire of the Spirit for Self-expression. By the nature of the case, the conception of the existence of any antecedent conditions is impossible; and so we see that creation from within (as distinguished from construction from without) has the entire absence of predetermining and limiting conditions as its distinguishing characteristic.

Then our thought, *inspired by the promise*, is, so to say, reflected back into the mind of the Universal Spirit in direct relation to ourselves and thus becomes part and parcel of the Self-realization of the Spirit in connection with ourselves personally, thus bringing about a working of the creative Law of Reciprocity from the standpoint of our own individuality; and because the activity thus called forth is that of the Original Creative Energy, the First Cause itself, it is as unhampered by antecedent conditions as was the original cosmic creation itself.

I have gone more fully into this subject in my *Creative Process in the Individual*, but I hope I have now said sufficient to make the general principle clear and to show that the Bible promises are nothing else than the statement of the *essential creativeness* of the All-originating Spirit when operating in reciprocity with the individual mind. If we believe in the power of Affirmation, then trust in the Divine promise is the strongest affirmation we can make. And if we believe in the power of Denials, then such a simple trust is also the strongest denial we can make, for, being absolute confidence, it constitutes an emphatic denial of any power, whether in the visible or the invisible, to prevent the fulfillment of the promise.

It is for this reason that the Bible lays such stress on belief in the Divine promises as the way to receive the blessing. The Bible was written for the benefit of *any* reader, whether learned or unlearned, and takes into consideration the fact that the latter are by far the more numerous; therefore it reduces the matter to its simplest elements: Hear the Promise, Believe it, and Receive its fulfillment.

The fact that the statement of any truth has been reduced to its simplest terms does not imply that it cannot stand the test of investigation; all that it implies is that it has been put into the best shape for immediate use alike for those who are able, and for those who are unable, to investigate the underlying principle. We press the button and the electric bell rings, whether we are trained electricians or not; but the fact that the bell rings for those who know nothing about electricity does not hinder the investigator from learning why it rings. On the other hand, the greatest electrician does not have to go through the whole theory of the working of the current when he rings at the door of your house, which would be inconvenient to say the least of it; and still less does he have to solve the ultimate problem of what electricity actually is in itself, for he knows no more about that than anybody else.

And so in the end he has to come back to the same simple faith in electricity as the man who does not know the difference between the positive and negative poles of a battery. His greater knowledge ought to *extend* his faith in electricity, because he knows it can do much greater things than ringing a bell; and in like manner any clearer insight we may gain into the *modus operandi** of the Divine promises should increase our trust in them, while at the same time it leaves us just on the same level with the most ignorant as to what the Divine Spirit actually is in itself.

We all alike have to come back to the standpoint of a simple faith in the vitalizing working of the energizing power, whether God or electricity, therefore the Bible simplifies matters by bidding us take this ultimate position as our starting-point, and not say, "I am confident because I know the law," but "I am confident because I know in whom I have believed."

I think some such considerations as these must have been at the back of St. Paul's mind, making him draw that distinction between Law and Faith which runs through all his Epistles. It is true he is, in the first instance, speaking of the ceremonial law of the Mosaic ritual, for he was addressing Jews for the most part; but if we reflect that reliance on that ceremonial was only one particular mode of relying upon knowledge of laws, we shall see that the principle is applicable to all laws; and moreover the original Greek word used by St. Paul implies law in general, thus giving a scope to his argument which makes it as applicable to ourselves as to Jews.

*"Method of procedure"—*Ed.*

And the point is this: laws are statements of the *relations* of certain things to certain other things under certain conditions. Given the same things and the same conditions, the same laws will come into play because the same relation has been established between the things; but this is exactly the sphere which excludes the idea of original creation.

It is the sphere of science, of analysis, of measurement; it is the proper domain of all merely constructive work; but that is just what original creation is not. Original creation is not troubled about antecedent conditions; it creates new conditions, and by doing so establishes new relations and therefore new laws; and since the declared purpose of the Bible is to bring us into a new order, in which all that is meant by "the Fall" shall be obliterated, this is nothing else than a New Creation, which indeed the Bible calls it.

Therefore our knowledge of particular laws, whether mental or material, is of no avail for this purpose, and we have to come back to the standpoint of simple faith.

I do not wish to say anything against the knowledge of particular laws, either mental or material, which is useful in its way; but what I do want to emphasize is that this knowledge is not the Creative Power. If we get hold of this distinction, we shall see what is meant by the promises contained in the

Bible. They are statements of the original creating power of the Spirit as it works from the standpoint of a specific personal relation to the individual, which relation is brought about by the expectant attitude of the individual mind, which renders it receptive to the anticipated creative action of the Spirit; and it is this mental attitude that the Bible calls Faith.

Seen in this light, faith in the promise is not a mere unreasoning belief, neither is it in opposition to law; but on the contrary, it is the most all-embracing conclusion to which reasoning can lead us and the channel through which the Supreme Law of the Universe—the Law of the creative activity of the All-originating Spirit—operates to make new conditions for the individual. It is not trying to make yourself believe what you know is not true, but it is the exercise of the highest reason based upon the knowledge of the highest truth.

The Divine promise and the individual faith are thus the correlatives of each other and together constitute a creative power to which we can assign no limits. When we begin to apprehend this connection of Cause and Effect, we see the force of the statements made by the Divine Master: "All things are possible to him that believeth"; "Have faith in God and nothing shall be impossible unto you"; and the like.

If we attribute any authority whatever to His sayings, we are justified by them in affirming that there is no limit to the power of faith and that His declarations on this subject are not mere figures of speech, but statements of the special and individual working of the Creative Law of the Universe.

Viewed in this light, the Bible promises assume a practical aspect and a personal application, and we see what is meant by being Children of Promise. We are no longer under bondage to Law—that is, to those laws of sequences which arise from the *relations* of existing things to one another—but have risen into what the Bible tells us is the Perfect Law, the Law of Liberty; and so according to the symbolism of the two representative mothers, Hagar and Sarah, we are no longer children of the bondwoman but of the free (Gal. 4:31).

Only, to be "heirs according to promise" we must be descendants of Abraham. I am not prepared to say that the majority of readers of this book are not so literally, though they may not be aware of the fact; but that is another branch of the subject with which I may deal in a subsequent volume.*

But setting aside this historical question, let us here consider the question of spiritual principles.

*Troward earlier addressed this matter at the very end (Ch. 12, "Salvation Is of the Jews") of *The Doré Lectures*, p. 206 of *The Edinburgh & Doré Lectures* (DeVorss ed'n; pp. 108, 109 of earlier ed'ns of *The Doré Lectures*).—*Ed.*

On this point the teaching of the Bible is very plain. It is that they are children of Abraham who are of the faith of Abraham; they are his seed according to promise—that is, they are living by the same principle which is set forth as forming the groundwork of Abraham's life: "Abraham believed God, and it was counted unto him for righteousness" (Rom. 4:3).

Now what will be the fruit of such a root? It must necessarily produce two results in our inner life: Restfulness and Enthusiasm. At first sight these two might appear opposed to one another, but it is not so, for Enthusiasm is born of confidence and so also is Restfulness. Both are necessary for the work we have to do. Without Enthusiasm there can be no vigorous work; even if attempted, it would only be done as task-work, something which we had to grind at compulsorily, and though I would not deny that a certain amount of good and useful work may be done from a mere sense of obligation, still it will be of a very inferior quality to what is done spontaneously for love of the work itself.

Take the case of the poor artist who is the slave of the dealer and has to labor from morning to night to turn out scores of little potboilers by a more or less mechanical process. If he be a born artist, the fact will assert itself in spite of the conditions, and even the potboilers will have some degree of merit. But put the same man in more favorable circumstances where he is no longer restricted by trade requirements, but is allowed to give full scope to his genius, then the artist in him rises up, he gives up* his own vision of nature, and masterpieces come from his brush.

This is because he is now working from Enthusiasm and not from Compulsion. It is also because he is working with a sense of Restfulness; he is no longer obliged to turn out so many potboilers per week to meet the demands of the petty dealer but can take his own time and choose his own subject and treat it in his own way.

Then the business side of his work will be negotiated for him by the big dealer, the man who also is an artist in his own way and knows the difference between the productions of spontaneous feeling and mere mechanical dexterity, and who finds his own profit in helping the artist to maintain that freedom from anxiety and the sense of compulsion without which such high-class works as the big dealer's business depends on cannot be produced.

Now this is a parable. God is the big dealer, and his best work through man is done for love and not by compulsion; and the more we realize this, the

* = "Serves up" —*Ed.*

better work we shall do. Am I irreverent in comparing God to some great picture-dealer of worldwide reputation and saying that he too gains his profits in the transaction? I think not; for Christ himself tells us of the master who looked to receive a profit out of his servants' work, and I have only clothed the old parable in modern garb and colored it with a familiar coloring.

And we may carry the simile yet further. The great dealer knows how to place the masterpieces in which he deals, he is in touch with connoisseurs with whom the artist cannot come in contact; and if the artist had to attend to all this, what would become of his creative vision?

How do you manage to paint such exquisite pictures? it was once asked of Corot, and he replied, "Je rêve mon tableau, et plus tard je peindrai mon rêve." There spoke the true artist, "I dream my picture, and afterwards I paint my dream." The true artist dreams with his eyes open, looking at nature, and it is because he thus sees the inner spirit of her beauty through its external veil of form that he can show others what they could not see, unaided, for themselves. This is his function, and the large-minded dealer enables him to perform it by taking the business side of the matter in hand in a generous spirit combined with a shrewd knowledge of the market, and so leaves the painter to his proper work by seeing his vision of nature and interpreting it by his individual method of interpretation.

So with the Divine Healer. He knows the ropes, he has command of the market, and he will deal in a liberal spirit with all who place their work in his hands. Let us, then, do diligently, honestly, and cheerfully the work of today, not as serving a hard taskmaster, but in happy confidence, and day by day hand it over to the Loving Creating Spirit who will bring out connections we had never dreamt of, and open up fresh avenues for us where we saw no way. You are the artist, and God is your honest, appreciative, and powerful Dealer.

But what else is this except exchanging the burden of Law for the peaceful liberty of Faith in the Divine Goodness, the All-givingness of the Heavenly Father? To attain this is far better than puzzling our brains over abstruse questions of theology and metaphysics. The whole thing is summed up in this: if you take your own knowledge of law as the starting-point of the creative action in your personal life, you have inverted the true order, and the logical result from your premises will be to bring the whole burden upon yourself like a thousand of bricks; but if you take the All-givingness of the Creating Spirit as your starting-point, then everything else will fall into a harmonious order, and all

you will have to do is to receive and use what you receive, asking the Divine guidance to use it rightly.

You throw the burden on whichever side you regard as taking the initiative in your personal creative series. If *you* take it, you make God a mere impersonal force, and ultimately you have nothing to depend upon but your own unaided knowledge and power. If on the other hand you regard God as taking the initiative by an All-givingness peculiarly connected with yourself, then the action is reversed and you will find yourself backed up by the Infinite Love, Wisdom, and Power.

Of course there is a reason for these things, and I have endeavored to suggest a few thoughts as to the reason; but the practical advice I give to each reader is: stop arguing about it. Try it, my boy; try it, my dear girl—for the promise is: "Let him take hold of my strength that he may be at peace with me, and he shall make peace with me" (Isaiah 27:5).

CHAPTER 14

The Spirit of Antichrist

When we have realized the essential nature of any principle, we can form a pretty fair guess as to the general lines on which it will show itself in action, whether in individuals, or institutions, or nations, or events. The evolution of principles is the key to all history in the past, and similarly it is the key to all the history that is to come; therefore, if we grasp the significance of any principle, though we may not be able to prophesy particular events, we shall be able to form some general idea of the sort of developments its prevalence must give rise to.

Now all through the Bible we find the statement of two leading principles which are diametrically opposed to one another: the principle of Sonship or reliance upon God, and its opposite or the denial of God, and it is this latter that is called the spirit of Antichrist.

This spirit, or mode of thought, is described in the second chapter of the second epistle to the Thessalonians and the fourth chapter of the first epistle to Timothy; and its distinctive note is that it sets itself up in the temple of God, placing itself above all that is worshiped, and a similar description is given in Daniel 11:36–39.

The widespread development of this inverted principle, the Bible tells us, is the key to the history of "the latter days," those times in which we now live, and the prophetic Scriptures are largely occupied with the struggle which must take place between these opposing principles. It is impossible for the two to amalgamate, for they are in direct antagonism; and the Bible tells us that, though the struggle may be severe, the victory must at last remain with those who worship God.

And the reason for this becomes evident if we look at the fundamental nature of the principles themselves. One is the principle of the Affirmative and the other is the principle of the Negative. One is that which builds up, and the other is that which pulls down. One consents to the initiative being taken by that Spirit which has brought all creation into existence, and the other bids this Spirit take a back seat and denies that it has any power of initiative. This is the essence of the opposition between the two principles. Whatever the one affirms, the other denies; and so, since no agreement is possible, the conflict between them must continue until one or the other gets the final victory.

Now if the spirit of Antichrist is what the Bible describes it, we cannot shut our eyes to the fact that it is now present among us. St. Paul tells us that it was already beginning to work in his day, only that at that time there was a hindrance to its fuller development; but he adds that when that hindrance should be removed, the development of the spirit of Antichrist would be phenomenal.

Various commentators on this text have explained the hindrance alluded to by St. Paul to have been the existence of the Roman Empire, and no doubt this is true as far as it goes. In this passage (2 Thess. 2:1–12) St. Paul reminds the Thessalonians of something he had *told* them on the subject—that is, something he had communicated verbally, and not in writing—regarding the falling away which would take place before the resurrection. He says, "Remember ye not, when I was yet with you, I told you of these things? And now *ye know* what withholdeth that he might be revealed in his time."

The very earliest traditions tell us that what St. Paul had then verbally explained to the Thessalonians was that the Roman Empire as then existing must pass away before these further developments could take place; but he was careful not to put this in writing lest it should expose the Christians to additional persecution on the charge of being enemies to the state.

The tradition that this was what St. Paul had told the Thessalonians is by no means a vague one. We first find it mentioned by Irenaeus,* the disciple of Polycarp,† who was himself the disciple of St. John; so that we get it on the authority of one who had been instructed by a personal friend and acquaintance of the apostles, and we may therefore feel assured that in this tradition we have a correct statement of what St. Paul had said regarding the nature of the hindrance to which he alludes in this epistle.

The existence of the Roman Empire, then, was doubtless the outward and immediate cause of this hindrance to the coming of Antichrist; but we must remember that at the back of the external and visible circumstances which are instrumental in the history of the world there are mental and spiritual causes, and so the matter goes further and deeper than any existing political conditions. It is a question of *spiritual* principles, a question of *causes*;

*(c. 120-140 to c. 200-203) Greek prelate—*Ed.*
†(2d century A.D.) Greek Christian martyr—*Ed.*

and so long as any given cause is at work, its effects will continue to show themselves, though the particular *form* they will assume will vary with the conditions under which the manifestation takes place.

Therefore we may look deeper than the political conditions of St. Paul's time to find the spiritual and causal nature of the hindrance to which he alludes. He tells us that at the time when he wrote, the spirit of Antichrist was already working, but that its complete manifestation was delayed till a later period by reason of a certain impediment which would be removed in due time; and a comparison of his statement with that of St. Peter in the third chapter of the second epistle shows that the removal of this impediment and the full manifestation of the spirit of Antichrist were to be looked for in the time of the end.

Now Daniel says the very same thing (Dan. 12:1-4), and he points out the marks by which the time of the end is to be recognized. They are two: "Many shall run to and fro, and knowledge shall be increased"; and if this is not an accurate description of things at the present time, well—I leave the reader to fill in the blank. We may say, then, that the time when the hindrance to the manifestation of Antichrist is to be removed is a time when knowledge has been increased; and if we reflect that the whole matter is one of spiritual powers, is it not reasonable to suppose that the hindrance which in St. Paul's time prevented the fuller development of the spiritual power of Antichrist was ignorance of the nature of spiritual power in general? Now this knowledge is becoming more and more widely diffused, and consequently the danger of its inverted application is today far greater than in St. Paul's time; and therefore the more we realize what potentialities open before us, the more it behooves us to be on our guard lest we regard them in such a way as to take the place of God in the temple of God.

It may, or may not, be that "the Man of Sin" exhibiting himself as God in the Temple of God is to be understood as an actual ceremony taking place in an actual building; though even this is not altogether inconceivable if we recollect that during the French Revolution a notorious actress was enthroned upon the high altar in the Cathedral of Notre Dame as the Goddess of Reason and received the public adoration of the official representatives of France. What has been may be again, and we know that history repeats itself; but I think we have to look for something more personal and powerful than any theatrical exhibition of this kind.

If we search the Scriptures, we shall find that the real Temple of God is Man. When Christ said, " 'Destroy this temple, and in three days I will raise it up,' he spake of the temple of his body" (John 2:19–21); and again St. Paul says, "Know ye not that ye are the temple of God?" (1 Cor. 3:16). Moreover, the promise is, "I will dwell in them, and walk in them; and I will be their God, and they shall be my people" (2 Cor. 6:16), and so in many similar passages, a careful consideration of which leaves no doubt but that the true significance of "the temple" in Scripture is that of human individuality.

The meaning then becomes clear. The temple which is profaned is the innermost sanctuary of our heart, out of which come all the issues of our individual life: "as he thinketh in his heart so is he" (Prov. 23:7); and if this be true, then it is of the utmost importance who is enthroned there. Is it the All-originating Creative Spirit with its infinite love, wisdom, and power? or is it our personal knowledge and will? It must be one of the two. Which is it?

The difference is immense, and it consists in this: if our personal knowledge, wisdom, and will-power are the highest things we know, then we are left exactly where we were and are making no advance. We may, indeed, accumulate a certain amount of knowledge of the hidden laws of physical and psychic forces not commonly known to our fellow-men, which knowledge must necessarily carry a corresponding power along with it; but this only places us in a position where we more urgently need a higher knowledge and a higher wisdom to guide us.

The greater the power you put into anyone's hands, the more mischief will result if through ignorance of its true uses he misapplies it. He may understand the mere mechanism, so to say, of this power perfectly, so that he will know how to make it work. It is not on the mechanical side that the mistake will occur. But the mistake will be in the *purpose* to which the power is applied; and if that be wrong, the greater the power, the worse will be the results. You may teach a child to drive a motor-car, but unless you can at the same time invest him with powers of observation and caution and promptness of resource in emergency beyond his years, his driving will end in a smash.

Now it is just this inspiration beyond our natural acuteness, of foresight beyond our unaided vision, that we require for the really useful employment of any enhanced powers that may come to us as the result of our increasing knowledge; and this is not to be drawn from the knowledge of what we may call the merely mechanical working of the Law of Cause and Effect, whether on the side of the visible or of the invisible. *That* knowledge, taken by itself, is only the lower knowledge—learning, so to say, how to do the particular trick. But to make it of real value, we need to know not only *how* to do it, but *why* to do it. And since the only true *why* is the building up of a harmonious whole both in ourselves and in the race—a whole which, by an organic connection between the causes sown today and the results produced tomorrow, shall continually germinate into greater and greater fulness of joyous life—and since the production of such a continuously growing and rejoicing wholeness is the only reasonable purpose to which our knowledge and our powers, whether great or small, can be applied, how are we to get such an outlook into the unending future and into our present relations in all their ultimate consequences by our own personal knowledge however extended?

We are sowing causes all the time with only a very limited outlook as to what they will produce; but if we are conscious that we have submitted our action to the guidance of the Supreme Wisdom and Love, we know that we must be importing into it an adjustment to wholeness which will make it cooperative with the great purpose of the Universe.

We cannot grasp that purpose in all its details and infinite extent, but we can see that it must be an unending growth into ever increasing manifestation of the Life, Love, and Beauty which the All-originating Spirit is in itself.

That Spirit is in itself Unity, and its Self-expression is through its manifestation in Multiplicity; and the more clearly we see this, the more clearly we shall see that the way to cooperate with it is by seeking to make our own thought the channel of *its* Thought. But to do this is to recognize the presence of a Divine Intelligence guiding our thought and a Divine Power working through our actions; and this recognition, coupled with the desire that our thought *should* be thus guided and our actions thus vivified, is the very essence of Worship. It is the very opposite to the mental attitude which sets itself up as needing no guidance and no help from a higher source, and which denies the working of any higher power; and so worship becomes the foundation principle of the life. This does not mean a specific ceremonial observance, but the adoption of the *principle* of worship, which is the recognition of the true relation of the individual mind to the Parent Mind from which it springs.

If anyone finds that a particular ceremonial conduces towards this end, then that ceremonial is useful to him, but it does not follow that the same ceremonial is necessary for somebody else. It is just like water-color painting. One man requires to keep his paper dry through the progress of the work, while another paints entirely in the wet; yet if they are both artists, each will record his vision in a way that will unfold to the spectator some secret of nature's beauty. Each must use the means which at his present stage he finds most conducive to the end, only let him remember that it is the end alone which really counts.

Therefore it is that the Great Teacher laid down only one rule for worship—that it should be "in spirit and in truth." The essence and not the form is what counts, because the whole thing is a question of mental attitude. It is that attitude of constant Receptiveness which is the only possible *conscious* correlative to the infinite Divine Givingness. To attain this is conscious union with the All-creating Spirit.

The logic of it may be briefly put thus: we want to come into touch with the Power which originates the universe; but we cannot do this and at the same time disqualify it by denying that it continues to be originative when it comes in touch with ourselves. Therefore to be really in touch with it as the *originating* Power, we must let it lead *us* and not try to compel *it*; and to do this is to worship.

The mark of the opposite mental attitude is to take no heed of such a Guiding Power, and then the only alternative is to set one's self in its place. When we realize that spiritual causes are always at the back of external phenomena, and the more we come to see that particular causes can be resolved into variations of an ultimate cause, the more our intent to rule that ultimate cause must result in self-deification.

But the bad logic comes in in not seeing that the real ultimate cause must be *entirely originative*—that this is just what makes it worth seeking—and trying to deprive it of this power by attempting to compel it instead of looking to it for leading.

It is just here that those who realize the nature of spiritual causation are in greater danger than the mere materialist. There really is an unseen Force which can be controlled in the manner they contemplate, and their mistake is in supposing that this Force is the ultimate Creating Power.

I daresay some readers will smile at this, and I am well aware that it is quite possible to build up an apparently logical argument to show that what I am now speaking of is a merely fanciful idea; but to these I will not now make any reply—the matter is one requiring careful development, and a partial and inadequate explanation would be worse than useless. I must therefore leave its discussion to some other occasion and in the meanwhile ask my readers to assume the existence of this Force simply as a working hypothesis. In asking this I am not asking more than they are ready to concede in the case of physical science, where it is necessary to assume the existence of purely speculative conditions of energy and matter if we would coordinate the observed phenomena of nature into an intelligible whole; and in like manner I would ask the critical reader to assume as a working hypothesis the existence of an Essence intermediate between the Originating Spirit and the world of external manifestation.

The existence of such an intermediary is a conclusion which has been arrived at by some of the deepest thinkers who have ever lived, and it has been called by various names in different countries and ages; but for the purpose of the present book I think I cannot do better than adopt the name given to it by the European writers of the fifteenth, sixteenth, and seventeenth centuries. They called it "Anima Mundi," or the Soul of the World, as distinguished from "Animus Dei," or the Divine Spirit, and they were careful to discriminate between the two.

If you look in a Latin dictionary, you will find that this word, which means life, mind, or soul, is given in a twofold form, masculine and feminine, Animus and Anima. Now it is in the dual nature thus indicated that the action of spiritual causation consists, and we cannot eliminate either of the two factors without involving a confusion of ideas which the recognition of their interaction would prevent us falling into.

When once we recognize the nature and function of Anima Mundi, we shall find that, under a variety of symbols, it is referred to throughout the Bible and indeed forms one of the principal subjects of its teaching; but to explain these Bible references in detail would require a book to itself. In general terms, however, we may say that Anima Mundi is "the Eternal Feminine" and the necessary correlative to Animus Dei, the true Originating Spirit. It is what the medieval writers called "the Universal Medium" and is that principle which, as I pointed out in the opening chapter of this book, is esoterically called "Water."

It is not the Originating Principle itself, but it is that principle *through* which the Originating Principle operates. It is not originative but receptive, not the seed but the ground, formative of that with which it is impregnated, as is indicated by the old French expression for it, "ventre saint gris," the "holy blue womb"—the innermost maturing place of Nature; and its power is that of *attracting the conditions* necessary for the full maturing of that seed with which it is impregnated and thus bringing about the growth which ultimately culminates in completed manifestation.

Perhaps the idea may be put into terms of modern Western thought by calling it the Subconscious

Mind of the Universe; and if we regard it in this light, we may apply to it all those laws of the interaction between conscious and subconscious mentality with which I conclude most of my readers are familiar.*

Now the two chief characteristics of subconscious mind are its amenability to suggestion and its power of working out into material conditions the logical consequences of the suggestion impressed upon it. It is not originative, but formative. It does not provide the seed, but it causes it to grow; and the seed is the suggestion impressed upon it by the objective mind.

If, then, we credit the Universal Subjective Mind with these same qualities, we find ourselves face to face with a stupendous power which by its nature affords a matrix for the germination of all the seeds of thought that are planted in it.

Looking at the totality of Nature as we see it—the various types of life, vegetable, animal, and human, and the evolution of these types from earlier ones—we can only come to the conclusion that the Originating Mind, Animus Dei as distinguished from Anima Mundi, must in the first instance see things *generically*—the type rather

*On this subject I would refer the reader to my *Edinburgh Lectures on Mental Science*.

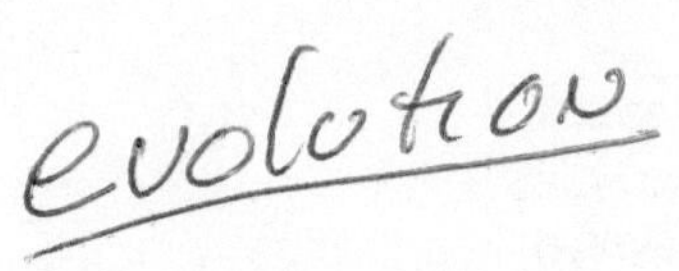

than the individual—much as Plato puts it in his doctrine of archetypal ideas; and so the world, as we know it, is governed by a Law of Averages which maintains and advances the race whatever may become of the individual.

We may call this a generic or type creation as distinguished from the conception of a specific creation of particular individuals; but, as I have explained more fully in my book *The Creative Process in the Individual*, the culminating point of such a generic creation must be the production of individual minds which are capable of realizing the general principle at work and therefore of giving it individual application.

Now it is the imperfect apprehension of this principle that causes its inversion. It is recognizing Anima Mundi without Animus Dei. And the more a man sees of the immense possibilities of his own thought and volition working upon Anima Mundi, while at the same time ignoring Animus Dei, the more likely he is to grow too big for his boots. He then logically has nothing to guide him but his own personal will; and with all the resources of Anima Mundi at his disposal, there is no saying to what extremes he may not go. "L'appétit vient en mangeant,"* and the more power he gets, the more he

*"Appetite comes from eating"—*Ed.*

will want; and the more his desires are gratified, the more he will become satiated and require fresh stimulus to his jaded appetites.

This is no fancy picture. History tells us of the Emperor Tiberius offering a great reward to anyone who would discover a new pleasure, and Nero burning Rome for a sensation. Picture such men in possession of a knowledge of psychic laws which would place all the powers of Anima Mundi at their disposal, and then imagine, not one such, but hundreds or thousands combining in some common enterprise under the leadership of some preeminently gifted individual, and recollect in this connection the accumulated power of massed mental action—and what must the result be? Surely just what the Bible tells us: the working of all sorts of prodigies which to the uninstructed multitude must appear to be nothing else than miracles.

The knowledge, then, of the enormous possibilities stored up in Anima Mundi, or the Soul of Nature, is the great instrument through which the power of Antichrist will work. It is, indeed, the acquisition of this power that will more and more confirm him in his idea of self-deification; and note that though for convenience I use the singular pronoun, I am speaking of a class—that is, of all who do not offer to God the sincere worship of trust in the Divine Love, Wisdom, and Power. I use the name Antichrist as that of a class, and one which seems likely to be widespread before long, though this in no way excludes the possibility of some phenomenally powerful leader of this class attaining to a preeminence which will make him the typical manifestation of the principle of self-deification.

Antichrist, whether as class or as individual, has attained to the recognition of a great universal principle, which I have endeavored to set forth in this and other books: the principle of the introduction of "the Personal Factor" into the realm of unseen causes. He has laid hold of a great truth.

All progress beyond the merely generic working of the Law of Averages is to be made by the introduction of the Personal Factor; but the mistake which Antichrist makes is that he cannot see any personality but his own. He sees the Soul of Nature and the power of its responsiveness to the Personal elements in the mind of man, and he sees no further. Therefore, after his own fashion he recognizes a spiritual power of mere *forces*, but he does not recognize beyond this the presence of "the God of gods" (Dan. 11:36-38). Logically, therefore, he becomes to himself *the* Person. He rightly says that the Law of Cause and Effect is universal and that the expansion of this law to the production of hitherto unknown effects depends upon the introduction of the personal factor; but he does not understand the reinforcement of the individual human personality by a Divine Personality, the recognition of which would bring in that principle of Worship which from the standpoint of this imperfect assumption of premises he logically denies.

To this power based upon self-deification there is opposed the opposite power based upon the worship of God; and the fact to be noted is that they are both using the same instrument. Both work by the power of the personal factor acting upon the impersonal Soul of Nature. The Anima Mundi itself is simply neutral. It is responsive to impression and generative of the conditions corresponding to the seed sown in it; but being entirely impersonal, it is without any sort of moral consciousness and will therefore respond equally to the impress of good or of evil.

Therefore in estimating the final result, Anima Mundi *may be entirely eliminated from our calculations*. To put it mathematically, if Anima Mundi be represented by the same quantity on either side of the equation, it may be struck out from both sides, and then the real calculation will involve only the remaining factors. In the case we are considering, the only other factor is that of Personality, and consequently the ultimate question at issue is this: on which side is the greater force of Personality?

The answer to this question is to be found in the

Cosmic Creation. We are part of that creation; our personality is part of it. Our personality proceeds by derivation from the All-originating Spirit, and therefore, logically, that Spirit must be the Infinite of Personality.

It is true we cannot analyze or fathom the profundities of that Spirit, and from this point of view we may speak of it as "the Unknowable"; and so we may not be able to define what the All-creating Spirit's consciousness of Personality may be to itself; but unless we entirely deny our derivation from it, must it not be clear that it must contain the infinite potential of all that can ever constitute personality in ourselves? And if this be so, then the growth of our own personality must be proportioned to the extent to which this potential flows into us; and to adopt the receptive mental attitude towards our Creator which will allow of such an inflowing is to take that attitude of Worship which Antichrist denies. Therefore the greater power of Personality is on the side of the worshipers of God.

Then, if this be so, their control over the powers of the unseen is greater than that of Antichrist, but they do not seek to control those powers in the same way that he does. He knows no personality but his own, and so he seeks to gain this control by his own knowledge of particular laws and by his own force of will and is thus limited by the capacities of his own personality, however extensive they may be. His method is to *consciously* control Anima Mundi for his own purposes by his own strength.

Those on the opposite side do not thus seek to subject Anima Mundi to their personal will. Many, perhaps the majority of them, do not even know that there is any such thing as Anima Mundi, and so they rely on a simple trust in "the Father." And those among them who do know it know also that the worshiper of God may entirely eliminate it from consideration, as I have already said, and so they also rely upon simple trust in "the Father"; the only difference being that, knowing something of the nature of the medium through which the unseen powers are working on *both* sides, and that the ultimate question is only that of Personality, they should have a yet stronger faith than their less instructed brethren, though in kind it is still the *same* faith—that of the Son in the Father.

Whether, then, instructed in these matters or not, the worshipers of God will by their very faith and worship be exercising a constant influence upon Anima Mundi, attracting all those conditions which must tend to their final victory over the opposing force.

Their worship enshrines the All-creating Spirit in their hearts, and their thoughts of him and desires towards him go forth into the Soul of Nature, impregnating it with the seed of the good, the beautiful, and the life-giving, which must assuredly bring forth fruit in its own likeness in due time.

Their method may not produce the sensational effects which may, perhaps, be produced by their opponents when the development of psychic forces reaches its climax, but in the end all such temporary wonders will be swept away by the overflowing of power which must result when Anima Mundi becomes permeated by Animus Dei, not merely as now in the generic sense of the maintenance of the world, but also in the specific sense of the introduction of the Personal Factor in its complete Divine manifestation.

Thus it will be seen that in its grand delineations of the closing scenes of the present age, the Bible nowhere departs from the universal law of cause and effect. There is a reason for everything if we can only penetrate deep enough to find it; and the laws of causation with which we are gradually gaining a better acquaintance in the realm of our own mentality are the same laws which in their wider scope embrace nations and make history.

When we see this, the why and wherefore of even that great climax of the present age which the Bible sets before us becomes intelligible. We may not be able to predict specific events, but we can recognize the development of principles, and so we see more clearly the meaning of those inspired prophecies which would otherwise be enigmatical to us.

Then when we see that these prophecies are in no way isolated from the natural laws of the universe, but rather are based upon them and are in fact the description of those very laws operating in their widest field of action on the human plane, we shall feel the more confidence in those hints of *definite measures of time* which they afford us.

This is a very important part of their message, and though we may not be able to reckon the precise day or year, we may yet come to a very close approximation of our present whereabouts in the chronological calendar, and there are many indications to show that we are very rapidly approaching that climax which the Bible calls the end of the age.

This, however, is far too large a question for me to open up in these concluding pages, and perhaps it may be my privilege to treat of it at some future time; but I have endeavored here to offer some suggestions of the general lines on which the Bible student may intelligently approach the subject, realizing the close connection that exists between the Bible teachings regarding the forgiveness of sin, the spirituality of worship, the development of personality, and the originative action of the All-creating Spirit. These are all parts of one great whole and cannot be dissociated. To dissociate them is to pull down the edifice of the Divine Temple; to realize their unity is to build up—that true Temple of God which is the Individuality of Man made perfect by the indwelling of the Holy Spirit.

IT SHALL COME TO PASS THAT WHOSOEVER SHALL CALL ON THE NAME OF THE LORD SHALL BE SAVED.

HIM THAT COMETH TO ME I WILL IN NO WISE CAST OUT.

MARANATHA*

*A Grecized form of Aramaic occurring in 1 Corinthians 16:22 and most commonly translated "Our Lord has come" —*Ed.*

science falls in the domain
of "constructive work" p. 306-307
"facts" defined 307

"The Universal Life Principle, as such, finds expression as much in one form as another, and is just as active in the scattered particles that once made a human body as it was in those particles when they cohered together in the living man..."

p. 199

on biological evolution on man an the human mind, see p 200.

perpetual life p 202

objective mind (physical instrument in contrast to subjective mind) is the brain p. 289

loss of objective mentality deprives us of the power of inaugurating fresh trains of ideas p. 290

how subjective mind may give rise to objective mind (even in absence of brain) p. 294